Abi Morgan

This is Not a Pity Memoir

JOHN MURRAY

First published in Great Britain in 2022 by John Murray (Publishers)
An Hachette UK company

3

Copyright © Abi Morgan 2022

The right of Abi Morgan to be identified as the Author of the Work has
been asserted by her in accordance with the Copyright, Designs
and Patents Act 1988.

Epigraph © Space Time Publications, 2011,
reproduced with kind permission of the Estate of Stephen Hawking
'Storm' © Tim Minchin, 2009
Dialogue on p.214 © Anthony Minghella, 1997,
Minghella Plays: 2 (*Contemporary Dramatists*), Methuen Drama,
an imprint of Bloomsbury Publishing Plc
'La Muerta', *Los Versos del Capitán* © Pablo Neruda, 1952 and Fundación
Pablo Neruda. Translation © Brian Cole, 1994, *The Captain's Verses*,
Anvill Press Poetry

A CIP catalogue record for this title is
available from the British Library

Hardback ISBN 978-1-529-38833-6
Trade Paperback ISBN 978-1-529-38834-3
eBook ISBN 978-1-529-38836-7

Typeset in Sabon MT by Palimpsest Book Production Ltd,
Falkirk, Stirlingshire

Printed and bound in Great Britain by Clays Ltd, Elcograf S.p.A.

John Murray policy is to use papers that are natural, renewable
and recyclable products and made from wood grown in sustainable
forests. The logging and manufacturing processes are expected to
conform to the environmental regulations of the country of origin.

John Murray (Publishers)
Carmelite House
50 Victoria Embankment
London EC4Y 0DZ

www.johnmurraypress.co.uk

For Jacob, Jesse and Mabel
. . . Deeply deeply

I regard the brain as a computer which will stop working when the components fail. There is no heaven or afterlife for broken down computers; that is a fairy tale for people afraid of the dark.

Stephen Hawking

I

It's dark and I'm pissed off. I've slept in the spare room again, so I am in no mood for chat. When I go in, I do my usual.

'Is it your head again? Have you taken paracetamol?'
But not in a nice way. In a way that he and I know will communicate my fatigue and frustration. The spare room is also his office. With an expensive pull-down bed. Meant for the occasional guest or my mother. Not for a week now. A week I've slept in the spare room because I snore. I keep him awake with my snoring. Or to be frank he keeps me awake with his snoring. Louder than mine. Though this is a point of dispute. A continual point of dispute. But for now, he's the one with the headache.

'I don't feel great.'

It's 7 a.m. and I want to drop our kids at school and get my coffee and go to work. The coffee that is the very expensive kind that I buy every day from the same, very expensive, coffee shop. Only today you have your hand on your forehead and you tell me it feels like there is a knife running from the top of your scalp into the back of your neck. So I'll get steroids from your consultant. Something I can do. Something I'm good at. And it's not that we're not used to this. It's not that this is not par for the course. I'll get a few hours' work in this morning, and then pick up your medication and get sushi for our son to celebrate his last GCSE, which is today, and then bring them back at lunchtime.

'Can you cope until then, Jacob?'

There's silence.

'You're a terrible nurse,' you reply.

And I think – you're right. I am a terrible nurse. I'm not built for this. A decade of rifling around for paracetamol and cold packs, and nights in the spare room. And then I lean in to kiss you and you say—

'What's it like to have everything?'

And I say,

'I don't have everything. Because you're not well.'

Buying sushi is a complicated business. I am nervous to stray from the path. No eel or anything that looks too like a slither of cold egg custard perched atop a small boat of rice. But still, I buy too much. And Wasabi peas, which I detest but which I know Jacob likes to flick into his mouth, lying on the sofa watching *The Simpsons* when I am working somewhere elsewhere in the house.

How can he live with such an unbearable lightness of being?

I like *The Simpsons*, but it never makes me laugh. My days are spent constructing story, manipulating truths, assimilating life into fiction. To be performed, acted in, filmed, shot. I watch movies and comedies with the precise and earnest eye of a surgeon. Not because I believe I am anything special. I am a writer. Although that would denote a certain level of expertise. But in truth I feel a fraud. Uneducated. Unbrilliant. At times, frankly, illiterate. I lie about the books

I've read. I am always trying *not* to be found out. If I am going to see a film I prefer to have read all the reviews and to know the plot beforehand. The joy for me is piecing together the narrative. I like being one step ahead of the audience, with my insider knowledge, like some second-hand moonlighting cop, sifting through the evidence, working out how it is done. How it has been crafted.

'Because she's actually a ghost,' I want to scream.

Or

'He's in the boot of the car.'

Of course, he's in the boot of the car.

I like to know how my story is going to end. And when I don't know, there is a kind of blind panic that unsettles, unnerves, terrifies me. Like a wet finger run around the top of the glass. I have to wait until the sound of this reverberating hum dissolves. Settles into silence again. And only then can I begin to breathe.

The chef rolls and slices and arranges sushi in flowered plastic trays with such grace. A master of his craft. I watch, waiting in front of the counter. I appreciate this. Afterwards I'll run to my office. I have missed the deadline. It's Friday and on Friday I am usually writing an email of apology that will fly into the arms of some small production company who will read it and sink a little, knowing they have to wait another weekend for that script that is already several weeks too late.

But today I have an excuse.

I have errands to run, steroids to pick up, a mission to accomplish.

I drive to Queen Square. A scrubby square of grass and rose beds marked out in black railings where the drunks and the dogs and the visitors and patients in wheelchairs and nervous parents walk, two steps behind their sick children, let out from Great Ormond Street for the afternoon for air and sun. Today office workers are flopped on the grass, cheek by jowl with dust-covered builders from a nearby construction site, swigging Coke and laughing in the heat.

It's June.

Did I say it was June?

I walk to the pharmacy inside the National Hospital for Neurology and Neurosurgery, a warren of doors and grubby plastic and disorientated old ladies gripping outpatient letters and nurses wheeling oxygen tanks. At the pharmacy I wait for the small white paper box of steroids that I hope will bring relief for the symptoms that Jacob has had for the last seven years, the MS that we try not to name, but which hovers dark and damp, like fret on a cold day, threatening to disrupt another evening, another holiday. And then I'm out, weaving my way back to the car.

Yes, it's June.

So, I must have picked up the steroids and after, after, that's when I drive to get sushi. For our son. To celebrate. Yes, I bought sushi after. Otherwise, it would have sat in a warm car. And I don't do that. I know I wouldn't have done that.

In the car, I slide the box of pills onto the dashboard. And suddenly I am crying.

Not crying. Sobbing.

Not sobbing.

Bawling.

Because I am tired of the years of steroids. And nights on

the spare bed. And the passive aggression that accompanies every exchange as we tread around, over and under this illness.

And I'm tired of pretending that any of this is OK.

It is not OK.

It is not OK.

The roar of a crowd and football commentary filters up from the living room TV before I have even opened the front door. Sliding down my bags, the dog helicopters like some crazed fan until I placate him with a pat and scratch. He loves me more than anyone, because I feed him and walk him, mainly.

I call out to Jesse, lost to FIFA, mid-match.

'Did you go up to see Dad?' I say.

Silence.

I take this to mean no.

I slide the sushi in the fridge, and then head upstairs to our bedroom. Four flights of stairs, and when I open the bedroom door, I am already congratulating myself on all I have achieved.

It is now 2 p.m., and I am incredible.

I am invincible.

I've got this nailed.

Did I say congratulations to my son?

The bed is empty, illuminated by the light from the bathroom.

Or was the bathroom door closed?

I turn and that is when I see you.

'Jacob?'

You are lying on the bathroom floor. A narrow tiled white space, that I complained reminded me of a sanatorium when it was finished. And which I got locked in only a week ago and had to shout down to you, banging the door with such violence that, two days later, I see I have left a dent in the wood. You rescued me.

The door is open.

'Jacob?'

I tell myself you are cooling down. The day is hot, and though the blinds are down, the room is always stifling. You must have come into the bathroom to cool down on the tiled floor. And have fallen asleep.

I lean over and try to rouse you. For a minute I can't decide if your lips are blue. Or are you wearing lipstick? And then I see that you have dried blood caked around your mouth.

'Jacob?'

Your eyes open. You stare at me.

'What?'

'Jacob – are you alright?'

'What? What? What? What? What?' you reply.

You are stuck. Your needle is stuck.

'Do you know what's happened, Jacob?'

'What?'

'Jacob, do you know who you are?'

'What?'

You raise a hand. I am sure you raise a hand, squinting a little, like a sunbather whose sleep has been disturbed by the shadow of looming clouds.

'Can you move?'

'What?' you reply.

I see now, you have bitten your tongue.

6

Standing on our landing, I realise I don't know who to call. Is it 999 or 911? Is 911 American? I call my friend Jacqui. Later I will tell people I called the ambulance first. But I didn't. I don't. I call Jacqui first.

I say, 'Jacob's collapsed. Jesse is downstairs. What do I do?'

'Call an ambulance,' she replies.

999. I call 999. I sit on the stairs, and turn my head, my eyeline now level with our bed. There is a large damp patch on the mattress. Is it blood or sweat? I think of the children when they were small. The nights we fumbled around in the dark together, stripping sheets after they'd wet the bed. You've pissed yourself.

You've pissed yourself.

'Hello, emergency. Which service do you need?'

I am not sure if this is what the woman on the other end of the line says. But it is what people say, isn't it? To be marked down, as I do with anything that I am writing, with an asterisk*. To be researched later. Facts to be checked later.

'An ambulance. I need an ambulance. My husband . . . partner . . . husband he's collapsed.'

'Is he breathing? Your husband, is he breathing?'

'He's not my husband . . . He's my . . . We live together.'

'And what's his name?'

For a minute I go blank. This is the man I love, the man I have known for nearly twenty years. The man who I have fought with and laughed with and loved with. The man who is never going to be the same again.

J . . . J . . . It begins with J—

'Jacob.'

I have attended twenty-two weddings in the eighteen

years I have lived with Jacob. And after every speech, every cheer, every coo of a passing bride, I have looked at Jacob and he has looked back at me, both of us knowing that this moment is a painful reminder of the fact that he has never wanted to get married.

To me.

'Is he breathing?' the voice on the other end of the line asks.

You spoke to me . . . you must be . . . You were able to speak to me.

'Yes . . . Yes. He's breathing,' I reply.

It is something I am very embarrassed about.

The not being married.

Which is ridiculous.

I am a woman who has a successful career, has won awards, owns property, has raised two children and lives with daily glimmers of happiness. I am a woman who intellectually, politically, philosophically knows that marriage is not an essential badge of honour. Yet still, if asked by a random stranger or parent at some obscure PTA event,

'How long have you been married?'

Still, it stings to reply,

'We're not actually married.'

'Oh, you said your husband.'

And that's the point. It's not the 'we're not married' bit. It's the fact that the word 'partner' never quite fits what we are. We are something else. And worse, the telling of the lie reveals that I am an interloper who has casually dared to take on the title of a married woman . . .

I always feel embarrassed. Caught out. Found out.

'. . . I just . . . I suppose . . . coming up to eighteen years . . .'

And every time I think I see it, the look of pity.

I am pathetic. I am pathetic.

'Yes . . . Yes, he's breathing,' I reply.

By the time I have come back into the room, you have managed to get yourself up and have staggered onto the bed. You are lying flat on your front, like some passed-out groom, face planted into the wet sheets, rambling, bemused that I have called an ambulance.

You tell me you just need Nurofen.

Did I get you your medicine? The steroids, did I pick them up from the pharmacy?

Perhaps I've left them on the car dashboard?

Yes – they're on the dashboard.

I think of running down to get them.

The air ambulance circling above the house feels a little dramatic, but I soon see we're well past Nurofen, well past steroids. They say they can't get you down the stairs and that you may need to be anaesthetised. A doctor and two other ambulance people have now arrived, and there is a paramedic on a bike. And two police officers. The atmosphere is almost jolly. They are nice. Everyone is so nice.

'Has he taken any pills?'

Scattered across the duvet and side table, like some addled rock star's bedroom, is a small apothecary of medications, blister packs of tablets, a chaotic rotation of over-the-counter drugs that you use to temper the ebb and flow of your MS. I realise they think you might have taken an overdose, and for a moment the world is turned once more upside down. Have you tried to kill yourself?

'No . . . I don't think so . . . not much . . . Only a couple of paracetamol maybe?'

You are roaring now. Writhing around on the bed.

'Perhaps you should wait outside,' one of them says.

I walk down the stairs, mulling on this.

Traditionally rock stars kill themselves at twenty-seven.

You will be forty-six in a few weeks.

Downstairs the first air ambulance man is admiring the posters on the wall of films I have written. He studied drama at university and wanted to be an actor in another life. He asks for a photo, standing by a framed poster of *Suffragette*. He has a beard. A thick beard. I take it with promises to circulate the photograph and to give him a rating, like giving stars to an Uber driver, and to encourage people to make donations to this desperately underfunded service.

I make promises I never keep.

Josh, my brother-in-law, Jacob's brother, has now arrived. And together with Jesse they have brought Mabel, our daughter, home from school, for cake and tea, reassuring her that all is well. Despite the fact that she is not stupid and has seen the air ambulance circling our house and can piece together that they are hiding something. But she is fourteen, and not yet cooked. Our baby. The baby of the family. And so we comfort her and lie.

One day in the future she will remind me of this.

*

Arghhh . . .

This will not do justice to the sound he is making. It is agonised. Tormented. Animalistic. He is gripping his head. It crosses my mind he might be faking it.

A few years before, he pulled a hamstring playing football and was carried back to our house and into our living room, where he writhed around on a brown leather circular pouffe that we bought for some different life. A massive blue purple bruise blushing on his thigh. Then, I internally rolled my eyes . . .

'You're such a fake.'

See . . . terrible, terrible nurse.

This time . . . This time is different.

Demonic.

They are trying everything. I can hear there is concern. Two-way radios. Machinery. The tear of plastic.

'Is he dying? '

I can hear them working on him.

'Fuck off . . . Fuck off . . . Fuck off . . . you cunt.' He is shouting now.

Later I will find he's ripped a socket from the wall.

In the emergency room, many hours later, I will remind him that he swore at everyone. He is mortified. They have had to sedate him to get him down the stairs. Jesse, our son, our boy on the edge of becoming a man, insisting that he can help carry his father.

'God . . . I didn't, did I? That's so embarrassing. I've got to apologise.'

He says this standing up, buck naked, but for a thin cotton

shift, open at the back, exposing a bare slit of flesh, oblivious to the fact that he's urinating all over the floor. It pools at my feet and I realise my trousers are wet. They've had to cut off his clothes and he is standing, like a man in the changing room of a department store, waiting for an assistant to return with the right trouser size, peering around the curtain, impatient and a little exposed.

We've been here for hours. In the end they blue-lit him in an ambulance, and the helicopter was sent away. I made small talk with the driver in the front. I can't remember if he/she was a man or woman, but as we pass the corner shop at the end of our road I quietly marvel at the world passing by, almost hoping I'll see someone I know. Someone who I could shout out to,

'I know this is happening . . . This is really happening.' And it is. It is happening. We are in UCH, one of the best training hospitals in the world. Josh spoke to Jacob's MS consultant and he advised that this was the best place for him to go. He will check in later. It must be a relapse. It must be that.

When I was a child, I would always love it when disaster happened. It meant that I could run into a room and say, 'The cat has died.' Or 'The gerbils have drowned.' I have a mawkish, voyeuristic relationship with mishap, life's brutal ability to upend destiny and disrupt the future you have marked out in your head. I like the look on people's faces when they stop and listen. I know if they look at their watch that, somehow, I have failed.

You are calming down, coming to, lying on a trolley, now parked in a different bay. Time has passed. You are thirsty and still a little delirious. But you are back. You are almost yourself again. You're not allowed water, so I wet a sponge and you suck on it. You still have blood on your lips. A young doctor, barely looking up from the paramedic's report, scribbles on forms, and whisks you off for an MRI. We sit, Josh and I, on scratched plastic chairs, dumbstruck and a little disorientated, eating sandwiches that Huw, my younger brother, has brought. Dorcas, my older sister, is at my house with Jesse and Mabel, my family already stepping up. Your family are waiting by the phone for an update, any news. I replay events over in my mind. When I look up again it is 11.23 p.m. Nine hours have passed.

A few nights before, you are working on lines.
You're an actor.
Did I say you're an actor?
You are shooting a couple of days before your collapse. Two scenes. And you ask me to help you. You must be struggling because I am usually the last port of call. Idle children and even the dog will be called upon to play the other parts before I am approached, because I will fidget and bristle and ask,
    'Is that the way you're going to do it?'
Often, we will have a row. That's normally the way it will go. But tonight, I feel honoured, grateful to be asked, keen to prove that I can do better at this. And you are keen to let me, both knowing that the need to redraw the lines of our relationship, to try and break old patterns and evolve new ones, has been recently discussed. I tend to hurry, push us on, in whatever task we are doing, an urgent need to

be always moving, a general fear of keeping still. It can ruin games of cards, leisurely holiday ambles and even conversation, so quick am I to finish a sentence and get onto the next thing.

I tell myself . . .

'Don't speak . . . Best behaviour. Don't blow this chance.'

I can do this.

I can be generous.

Supportive.

What you need.

Want.

It's a long speech . . . I think it's about communism . . . You are a revolutionary, in some TV series set in Israel . . . Or is it the part of George Orwell's agent? A single scene in a film where the camera will undoubtedly be on the handsome bankable lead throughout every one of your lines? I can't remember. Months after this has happened, I will search up the trailer of the film about Orwell on my laptop, just to see your face. You're good. You've grown into your skin. They've shaved your beard. I remember you came back saying how much you liked the make-up girls. But then, you like everyone on a set. You tell me it feels like home. You're fickle. The director is Polish, a woman, I think. You like her. You are happy.

In the scene, George Orwell crosses a restaurant floor. The room is all 1940s palms and cut glass and you will smile and shake his hand. And for a minute I will see you as you were before. Dynamic. Funny. Sweet, sweet man. The job is a leap for you. A good role. You get rabbis, terrorists and ageing depressed salesmen. And agents. You often get asked to play agents . . . with agency. But this,

this is a three-hander with the star. Later, when I actually see the film, a gripping, Stalin-era thriller that barely makes it onto Amazon, the camera even lingers a little on your face.

The night before shooting, you are word perfect, I know you are word perfect. You are brilliant. Yet every fourth line you suddenly drop a word. You fumble, leaning forward in the white leather chair in our living room. I am hunched over, feeding back the words, reading in the other parts.

'What's wrong with you tonight?'

It is funny.

We laugh, a lot.

I don't know that you have rung your consultant only a few days before. You have told him that you are experiencing '. . . incredibly scary symptoms', that you hide from me. You are losing words. You have electricity in your head. None of this . . . none of this you will reveal.

'Well, the good news is he has got a brain.'

The young doctor, the main registrar on call, is relieved, relieved enough for gags, this one I imagine he has used several times. You look up from the gurney, your scans now returned. The MRI looks fine. The rash that has appeared over the last week or so, the microscopic purple pin pricks dotting your back and neck, is still a mystery, but they will put you on an antiviral and antibacterial drip immediately. It's some kind of infection, they reassure us. Most probably an infection, so best to get ahead and treat you straight away. You'll stay in overnight on the infectious diseases ward. Josh and I are relieved, weirdly relieved. This conversation is almost normal. You're calmer, they've even given you a side room. I kiss you goodbye. You need to sleep . . .

'Sleep now. Let them work out what is wrong with you.'

But we are reassured, Josh and I, both reassured.

'You're going to be fine,' I tell myself.

Visiting hours start at 9 a.m.

'I'll be back first thing,' I tell him.

We head home and I fall into bed.

It is past 1 a.m.

Someone has changed the sheets, though the mattress still feels a little damp. The headboard is at a slight angle to the wall. Small clues that it is real, it happened, are like guide ropes amidst the blur. The plastic light switch, that controls the dimmer by my side of the bed, has pinged across the floor and is now resting on the side table. A pair of trousers, still scrunched in almost comic-like concertina on your side of the bed, where you stepped out of them the night before. There are still spots of dried blood on the herringbone tiles in our bathroom. A plastic cellophane wrapping from a medical dressing, gathering fluff on the carpet, gets stuck to my foot as I walk back across the room.

I sleep.

I sleep, in spite of it all.

At 4.30 a.m., the buzz of my phone wakes me. I pull on my clothes and drive back to the hospital. It is not yet dawn. When I get there, you're pacing, agitated, and you fall on me as I walk through the door.

'Thank God, you're here,' you say.

You're insistent. I need to call your agent. To tell her what is not quite clear. But you're back. You are still Jacob and this plea, though a little random, is almost plausible. I agree to call her, your agent, but I remind you that it's Saturday, not even 7 a.m. and not pressing. I am told by a passing nurse that the IV is kicking in.

'So why's his temperature still raised?' I ask.

You are moved again, to another side room, across another ward. By 9 a.m., you are calmer, though the painkillers are barely touching the headache, pounding just behind your left eye. You tell me this as you spoon hospital-issue yoghurt into your mouth. I need to track down someone, find out what is going on. Consultants come and go. One in particular, gnarly and seemingly a little disgruntled to be working on a Saturday, informs us, and the trail of blinking student doctors who loiter nervously by his side, that the tests are back. Good news again – meningitis and Hep A have now been ruled out. They'll do some more.

What's caused your collapse is still a mystery.

Your mother, sister, brother, father, visit in rotation, crowding around your bed, admiring the view – an undisturbed vista of the Euston Road. It all feels a bit of a lark now. There is even the World Cup on the TV. You smile, quietly enjoying the attention, in pretty good spirits, the cocktail of codeine and paracetamol offering a temporary high. The only cloud is that the seizure means you won't be able to drive for a year.

This pisses you off.

How you love to drive.

'I'll drive, babe,' a constant refrain as we head out to whatever party, dinner, play, car keys clutched in hand.

17

Not anymore. Not anymore.

'It's only a year,' I reply.

Looking out through the grey grime, the fog of pollution and pigeon shit blotting the window, I remember a drunken night, after one of those twenty-two weddings, of good friends, who were very much in love, when you carried me along the Euston Road, piggyback style, me, heels in hand. You flagged down a taxi, got me home, made me gulp down a glass of water, looking in on Mabel and Jesse in their bedroom, picked up earlier from the wedding reception by your mother while their parents partied on. Both asleep in their beds, drunk on wedding cake and caught in a tangle of duvet. I still have the photo of the two of us from that day. You in a suit, that is too big around the shoulders. Me in a coat, nipped in, back when I had a waist. We are different people. It is a different time.

'We are so lucky . . .' we told one another then.

Were we too smug?

With our cake and our kids and our weddings?

That photo on the mantelpiece will come to haunt me.

One night, I turn it to face the wall.

Sunday, Father's Day. You have been here two days, two nights, locked in UCH. The grapes and folded newspapers gathering on the side table and windowsill, give the room an air of normalcy. You have almost settled in. The children get to see you for the first time since your collapse. Mabel has made a card. Your headache is worse, but you like the book Jesse has brought you, about dinosaurs, I think. You leave it resting on the table, with the smoothies that family keep bringing, which you barely touch.

To be read later. To be drunk later.

Afterwards I take Jesse and Mabel for sushi and frozen yoghurt. We eat and laugh, punch drunk, sitting at a corner table, looking out over Warren Street.

They are relieved.

You are still Dad.

You are still funny.

It's going to be fine.

It is all going to be fine.

There's a school of thought that your rash might be some kind of Italian tick, possibly picked up during the May half-term break, possibly at the house we have built. You have built. Weeks and months of fixing and tile buying, the kids eating salami as it rains. No one told us it rains so much in Italy. In Puglia. Your baby. Your joy. A *trullo* on a square of earth, with olive groves, figs and lemon trees, a house family can all return to, with the plan one day to rent it out during the summer months. You come late to the week. You've been filming. Perhaps that was the Orwell film. You are relaxed and confident. The sun is shining. The grass is long. Filled with ticks.

In Italy we gorge on mozzarella, burrata the size of a baby's fist, thinly sliced meats, gelato and Toblerone, thick triangle slabs picked up from duty free. Over lunch, you look quizzical, watching Mabel serve herself from a plate of cheese and cold meats.

'That's not how you eat burrata,' you say.

You are unsettled, that she has dared to cut herself a small piece.

'How do I eat it, Daddy?' Mabel replies, smiling, a little bemused.

You pick up the whole burrata, huge and milky and dripping, balancing it on a tiny piece of bread, and bite, almost indignant.

You are ridiculous. It is ridiculous.

We laugh at you and for a moment there is a look of stunned affront. And then it is as if you come to and you join in our laughter.

Rewind.

Now, lying in our bed, I think again about your earnestness, the way you carefully raised the burrata to your lips. The flicker of embarrassment as we laughed, and your attempts to join in, not to be left behind, to be in on the joke, your shame hurriedly packed away. I'm trying to work out this plot, to piece together each scene and follow the strands of this unfolding story. I look up Lyme disease and Italian ticks. There are over forty species and the tick fauna in Italy is one of the most diverse in Europe. The *Ixodes ricinus* tick is one particular nasty motherfucker. I reassure myself these are found mainly in the Lombardy region.

But still—?

Google is a very bad thing.

'What am I?'

It is Monday. You have been at UCH for nearly three days.

'What do you mean, what am I?' I reply, confused.

'You're a father, a partner, a brother, a son, a friend, an actor . . .'

You are staggering now between your bed and the compact

corner bathroom in the side room that you have not yet left.
You try to pee.
You can't.
You are restless.
The pain in your head is worse.

'What is my purpose?'

'My duty?'

'Why am I here?'

'Where is my honour?'

'Am I here to serve?'

'Serve what?' I ask. 'Serve who?'

On TV, Russia is beating Egypt 3–1. I try to distract you with football. Anything. You can't remember who gave you the dinosaur book. I tell you it was Jesse the day before. You read the inscription he wrote inside, meticulously. You look at me blankly and ask for more morphine. The pain in your head is getting worse.

'Something's not right, Abi. Something's not right.'

They move you out of the room and onto a ward. This seems a backward step.

Or maybe a sign that you are getting better, even though I can see you are getting worse?

Something is not right.

Natasha, my sister-in-law, comes to visit the following day.

I have known her since she was a schoolgirl of sixteen. She has grown up alongside my children. She is strong and independent and my children's lovely aunt. But above all this she is Jacob's much-loved younger sister. Until now, she has not seen her brother in this increasingly disorientated state.

When I arrive, she is drained of colour, white as a sheet. We find her a chair and she slides down the wall, overwhelmed with shock. You are in a comatose state now, mute. Your head is a little turned, looking away. You are rapidly deteriorating. A nurse hovers and tells me you were too disorientated to be left alone last night.

What is happening?

You are changing, transforming, unravelling.

Three days ago, you were talking, they were doing more tests.

Now . . .?

Now you are silent, staring, refusing to communicate.

I want to wake up.

The world is as it was, yet everything is moved a little to the left.

Walls sloping, floors sinking, back sliding down the wall.

Shock, the body's attempt to protect, is back. It slows time, insulates one from the unfolding chaos, submerges me, almost as if I am underwater, my life passing me by in a kind of muffled blur. I am back in our house, the day you collapsed, standing on the stairs, you in our bedroom, writhing on the bed, pulling out sockets from the wall. I'm a spectator of my life, horrified yet perversely still marvelling at the drama of it all.

'Argh . . .'

Only you're not screaming this time.

You're perfectly still.

Silent.

Vacating yourself.

Across the room, Anthony, a fellow patient with long dreadlocks, shouts at me, concerned and kind, telling me you have had a 'terrible night'. You'd been arguing loudly 'about Brexit' and you are 'refusing to eat'. I have a box of raspberries. I pop them one by one in your mouth and you silently chew and swallow, not looking at me, opening your mouth after each one like a baby bird, eyes fixed, barely tracking the players on the TV.

You've changed. Daily I watch you change.

Jesse arrives. I have tried to keep him away, but you've been here nearly five days.

'Hey Dad?'

You do not turn. You don't even look at him.

Someone scores a penalty. You don't react.

'Dad?'

You ignore him.

'Dad?'

It is heart-breaking.

'Man . . . You've got to eat,' Anthony yells from across the room.

Silence.

They still don't know what is wrong with you.

That night they move you to a different bay.

It is late 2000; I have the tail-end of a shitty cold. But a girlfriend, one of my best friends, is having a dinner, for a birthday. She is a very good cook and I like to eat. She is bold in her choices, of menu and guests. I drive over, weaving my way through the elegant grid of West London streets. A beautiful, miniature jewel box of a house, in a neat Georgian terrace, with faces, some familiar, some new, caught in candlelight and enticing conversation. A long table runs from living room to kitchen, covered with a tablecloth of newspapers and a mismatch of chairs, like some chaotic, brilliant Lewis Carroll high tea. I am out of my depth. There is an elegance to the way my friend lives, with which I cannot compete. I am awkward and overeager to please.

And I am getting over a cold.

Standing in the kitchen, a shaven-headed man walks in. I immediately peg you an out-of-work actor. You have questionable facial topiary, a Shakespearean beard. A thick green pullover, which I think to myself must be hot. But I don't notice you properly again until midway through dinner.

A runner of cooked prawns still in their shells has been spilled chaotically along the centre of the long table. We stand, cracking and peeling and fiddling to retrieve small pieces of fishy meat. It is decadent. Fun. Silly. Rich. These people are educated, privileged, sophisticated, bohemian. At some point, we are told to grab a chair, with the urgency of musical bumps at a kids' tea party.

Sitting opposite me is a young woman, getting very drunk. Let's call her Caroline. The tall, dark foppish man to my left ominously whispers she 'does something in TV'. He touches my shoulder, compliments me on my shirt, his finger running close to my collarbone, touching my skin. Years later I will realise this was an attempt at a pass, and that, if I had had more confidence to see it for what it was, my life might have been completely different. The shirt is cheap and spotty with a bow tied close to my neck. On our second anniversary Jacob will admit that it made me look like an air hostess.

'What do you do?' Shakespearean beard is sitting opposite me.

Say it.

Say it.

I can say it.

I get paid now.

Almost paid now.

I can say it.

I am almost earning money. A decade of waitressing almost behind me.

'I'm a writer.'

'Not another fucking writer.' Caroline, the drunk girl, now seated to his right, is proving to be a real charmer.

'What the fuck do you write?'

You can do this. You can say this.

'I'm hoping to get the rights for an amazing book by Ruth Picardie?'

'Wow.' You smile. 'What for stage . . . TV?'

'For a film. I want to adapt it into a film,' I reply.

'Picardie. Isn't she the one who died?' the drunk girl butts in.

In my mind she says this, slopping her drink. In my mind. But then as I now know, the mind plays tricks.

'I read her column. Ruth's column. "Before I Say Goodbye,"' you reply.

'Yes, now collected into a book,' I reply.

'God . . .' The drunk girl looks to him to pour her more wine.

But you ignore her. You ignore her and look directly at me. Smiling, looking directly at me.

'They were brilliant.'

Ping.

There is this deep internal ping.

Perfectly crafted, poignantly revealing, 'Before I Say Goodbye' was a series of wittily written emails and columns first published in the *Observer* by Ruth Picardie as she dies of cancer in her house in North London.

And you have read them.

'I fucking hate those pity memoirs.' The drunk girl again.

'Why?'

You're still smiling, looking back at Caroline now, yet smiling. Caroline. Yes, that was her name. This drunk, obnoxious, wine-swilling girl. She may have been none of these things. But in my memory, Caroline smiles back at you, flirtishly. Maybe she even puts her hand on your arm, her gaze holding yours.

'Why share your fucking misery?'

'Who wants to read that?'

I am so embarrassed. I am found out.

'Me,' I want to shout. 'I want to read it. Me.'

But I don't. I go back to the man on my left. He has good hair. Thick hair. Genetically that would have been useful. Hair is notoriously thin in my family. And as I am talking to the good thick-haired man on my left, I can hear you arguing with her, charmingly, defending me.

It should be said I never got the film rights.

After, after candles have been blown, and cake has been eaten. After, when the music is louder, making the floorboards vibrate, I take my moment to leave.

A sister of an old friend and her boyfriend want a lift.

'Is there room for my friend? He was going to get a taxi.'

I can't remember answering, but I must have agreed to give him a lift because you are now sitting in my front seat.

You are still holding a bottle of beer and ask if I want a drink. I point out I am driving. I am not sure if you are pissed. But you are warm and funny and charming and you listen. I drop the other two off somewhere near Gospel Oak. I take a left onto the Holloway Road, by the Odeon cinema, not yet gentrified with waiter service and guacamole chips on boards and reclining seats, and, as I take a left, I'm laughing so much I momentarily lose my bearings, and gently you reach out a hand, touch the wheel,

'Steady.'

Ping . . . Ping . . .

We stop outside a pretty suburban house and you invite me in for a cup of tea. You're staying with your mother, the glass ornaments on glass shelves in the neat, cream living room the giveaway. I can't remember what we talk about. You're between jobs, assisting a friend who is shooting something.

An out-of-work actor.

'Of course,' I think.

We say goodbye, neither of us making a move, me tripping over the step, as I back out through the front door, flustered and nervously laughing, with no promise of ever meeting again.

Yet I drive home giddy, my flat, ten minutes away in a grubby part of north-east London that never comes up, Lubavitch Jews or prostitutes standing on every other street. It is a crisp dark night, 2 a.m. London is asleep. But as I take a right along an icy road I know well, I skid. The car goes round and round, like some cognitively slow Torvill and Dean, until it comes to an almost graceful stop, perfectly placed in the left lane, facing my way home.

In years to come, when I retell this story, I will catastrophise, the car spinning in a terrifying figure of eight.

'I could have been killed,' I will say.

'I could have been hurled into scrubland never to be seen again,' I will add.

'It's a miracle I survived, my life flashed in front of my eyes.'

And as the story grows I will tell myself it is a sign. When I eventually do get out of the car, I see I have laughed so much, I have peed a little on the seat.

The next morning, I call my girlfriend and tell her I have met the man.

The man.

By lunchtime, I have matched my first name with yours – Kri . . . Chef . . . Ski.

By evening, we are married with two kids.

I wait for your call.

You never call.

I call my friend, the sister of my friend, fake a story that I need your email address. Email is just coming in, sent and received on the bright blue blocky Apple laptop, more Fisher Price than iMac, that sits in a corner on my desk. You have asked if you can read one of my scripts, and I am keen to help a young out-of-work actor with aspirations to be a screenwriter. I can sense her smiling on the other end of the line, knowing this is a lie.

'No, I don't want his number,' I reply.

I need to write. I am better with words than in person, they are good at hiding my shattering lack of confidence.

I get it.

I email you.

Nothing.

A silence that is a deafening.

I am heartbroken. I am ancient. I am over the hill.

A few days later, I am working on my laptop at my desk and then suddenly from my inbox—

. . . Ping!

You are having another seizure. Tonic clonic seizure. They normally last one to three minutes. Over five, they are classified as a medical emergency. This one has come on suddenly, the consultant is trying to explain. They need to take you down for an MRI immediately. A swirling mob of IC consultants, doctors and nurses are surrounding you. A curtain is yanked, separating you from us. But I can see, as they pull it closed, that you are writhing, arching your back, as if mid-exorcism, screaming in agony. You have been in hospital for exactly seven days.

'Something is wrong, Abi. Something is wrong.'

I should have listened to you.

Why didn't I listen to you?

Seven days.

I have sat for seven days feeding you raspberries, not wanting to disturb the nurses, not wanting to try and pin one down as they flit past, to ask why they can't find out what is wrong with you. Then I remember Baz, a friend of Jacob's from university, a doctor, once told me that those who shout loudest are heard.

'Is he going to die?'

She is very pretty the consultant. Blonde. A nice woman. In another life, I would have liked to have been her friend.

'I have teenage children. I need to prepare them if he is going to die.'

Judith, Jacob's mother, is standing to my right. She is lost and anxious and so fragile, trying to keep up, trying to understand what is happening.

Later I will hate myself that she heard me ask this.

'I need to prepare them if he is going to die.'

The nice consultant's eyes fill with tears. Or I think they do. In my mind I am commending myself for my calm stoicism, my strength that is brave, so brave that I have moved her to tears.

She pauses, is trying to compose her words.

Shit, this is serious.

This is not a film . . .

If it was, I would have cut this scene.

'Yes. He could die. Imminently.'

You didn't die.

Some days.

Often.

There are days when I wish you did.

You had.

But—

. . . you—

. . . didn't—

. . . die.

You—

. . . do— . . . not—

. . . die.

2

'Fuck, I'd love to do that.'

A few months before you read somewhere that Richard Branson has a plan to send a rocket to Mars. For 250,000 dollars you can buy a ticket on the Virgin Galactic's spaceship. I am incredulous. I would rather stick pins in my eyes.

'Seriously?'

You are being serious.

'But there is no promise you'll come back?' I reply.

'And?'

'You'd never see us again. You'd never see your family. Or your friends,' I persist.

'Would that really be so bad?' You smile.

That smile. You're kidding, playing one of your games. But somewhere in the back of my mind, I know part of you believes it. Part of you would do it if you could. I find myself googling Virgin Galactic late at night. The website is impressive. The bearded Branson looking part mystic, part *Right Stuff*, standing on the tarmac, looking off into the middle distance, shot in side profile.

Virgin Galactic recognizes that the answers to many of the challenges we face in sustaining life on our beautiful and fragile planet, lie in making better use of space . . .

From space we are able to look with a new perspective both outward and back . . .

You have always wanted to go into space. A fascination that has spawned numerous birthday presents and stocking fillers. Freeze-dried space ice cream that we find, crushed and still in its silver foil wrapper, in the bottom of a stocking when we take them out the following year. One Christmas I buy you a telescope. A very expensive telescope. You show the kids the moon, spending hours getting the magnification just right so that they have a perfect view.

You are the adventurer in the relationship.

You are the fun.

When Jesse was first born, tiny, riding in a front-facing sling that you are proudly wearing, you are already planning. Trips to Costa Rica, Tokyo, San Francisco, Sydney. Some we will do, and some we won't. But I'm always hovering a few steps behind, agitated, the ying to your yang of fearlessness. Always waiting for something to go wrong. For disaster to fall. But it never did.

I would say,

'Do your shoelaces up.'

And you'd always ignore me. You would walk with them hanging, threatening to trip you up. You'd ride a Vespa, graduating to motorbikes, with the kids perched in seats on the back, so small their feet would barely touch the footrest, taking them to nursery and then school. And always, always with me watching, holding my breath, waiting for disaster, waiting for that call.

When did stories of disaster stop being something I

enjoyed and become something I feared? Because it never happened. I never got that call.

And I started to breathe. Started to breathe again.

When did I start to trust in that life?

'We are so lucky.'

Because I should never have done that. I should never have stopped waiting.

For it to come.

How could I have been so cocky?

This is not a pity memoir . . .

This is not a fucking pity memoir . . .

This is a pity of a memoir. This is a fucking pity of a fucking memoir.

An induced coma, also known as a medically induced coma, a barbiturate induced coma, or a barb coma, is a temporary coma (a deep state of unconsciousness) brought on by a controlled dose of a barbiturate drug, usually pentobarbital or thiopental.

After another week this is what they will do.

But for now you are back.

But not as you were.

You lived . . .

You lived.

Five days have passed since I pushed your consultant to tell me if you were going to die. Five days since we sat in the Caffè Nero across from UCH, barely talking, me and your family, eating dry biscuits and weak tea, and at one point I paced outside, calling anyone, calling no one. And then we got the call from the hospital. You are back. You are alive. You do not die. Your scans still look fine. It makes no sense.

You live.

But not as you were.

You are not as you were.

Five more days and you are unravelling a little more.

You have been here eleven days. Eleven days since I found you, eleven days since I bought sushi and planned for a summer that will not happen now.

They've put you in a side room, assigned a roster of agency nurses and a security guard by your door so you can be monitored twenty-four hours a day.

'Lately . . . likely. Lately . . . Likely . . . Likely . . . Not likely laaaakly laaakly.'

You turn to look at us.

'It's just a small thing laaaakly. Dya see? It's just: laaakly not likely.'

You are no longer silent. You talk, incessantly. You sit fixed in your bed, staring straight ahead. Word salad spilling, filling the room. We watch, like some kind of fascinated, horrified, terrified audience. Helpless. Impotent.

'D'ya see? It's just: laaakly not likely.'

You're working on your Yorkshire accent. A flash of a smile, you are amusing us. Deb, Josh's wife, sitting beside me, plays along.

'Laaakly, yeah it's laakly,' she replies.

You smile. I can see relief on your face. You are already heading towards the other planet. In your space rocket. Tapping at the radio, hoping someone can hear you. That someone will listen.

'We understand you. We can hear you.'

You look at us.

'We can hear you, Jacob,' we say.

'Saster. Disaster. Disaster. The worst,' you reply.

'Yes, it's the worst, Jake.'

'I love you, Jake. I love you,' I say.

I feel sick.

'Yup!' you reply, looking away.

'Is an Indian Indian? Is he Indian?'

'From the West Indies. I think he is from the West Indies.'
Justice, the name of one of the security guards, or perhaps
it was something else, we had talked, he had told me of
his childhood in Grenada. I say this hushed. You don't
care. Uninhibited. Desperate. Smiling but desperate. Still
speaking.

'Is India Indian? . . . Is an Indian interesting? . . . Ah
that's interesting . . . I get it.'
You start pointing.

'No no I get it now ahhhhh I see now I get it.'
You keep pointing, like an animated diplomat at a drinks
party, making small talk.

'Is Indian industry interesting? . . . Interesting industry
in India . . . Indian interesting listening? . . . Are you
listening? . . . Are you listening? . . . Are you listening?'
We tell you, we are listening.

'Yes, Jake. We are here. We are listening.'
You are relieved. You smile, eyes glazed. In your rocket,
heading somewhere else.
You raise your hand.

'High five.'
You high five Deb.

'High five.'

Then you high five me. It is a great moment. You are still here. Somewhere else. But still sending messages back.

'Yes, Jake. Yes, we hear you. We understand.'

You are calm now, relaxing back into your pillows at last. You suck your thumb. I kiss you and you look at the nurses.

'Lovely . . . Lovely . . . Lovely people.'

'Yes, everyone is very kind,' I reply.

And then you look at me, really look at me, shoulders raised, brows furrowed, like the lion in *The Wizard of Oz*.

'I get this shorty sharey feeling you know that sharey saucy shorty feeling do you know that saucy that short of saucy sharey, you know?'

Yes, we know. We understand you somehow. You are beautiful and it is heart-breaking, watching you soft like a child. And I have an urge to get you out of here, get you into a car, drive you home, help you up the stairs, back into our bedroom at the top of the house. I will take off the hospital-issue nightdress with its depressing dotted pattern and I will put you in pyjamas, pyjamas that you do not own, that I will find, miraculously clean and folded in a drawer. And you will climb into bed, and I will climb in next to you, spoon up close, press my knees against the cool of your shins, my face to your back, pull the duvet. And the world will be as it was.

Rewind.

Because I don't want this life that is coming, this frantic, terrifying detour, that shakes me to my core, gripping me with a terrifying churning motion sickness as life as we know it hurtles past.

This BC life – before collapse. This AD life – after disaster.

Saster. Disaster. Disaster . . . The worst.

It is the worst.

But more than this, much more than this . . . it is mainly sad.

You are hungry. Starving. We realise the nurses have been bringing you food but leaving it to go cold on the tray. It has been twelve days now. And no one has been feeding you. A shepherd's pie arrives and Josh spoons it into your mouth. You are ravenous. It is moving watching the care with which Josh feeds you. You are getting hotter. Your temperature is going up again.

You are going.

You are going . . .

You are going again.

'Get out of the fucking way. Get out of the fucking way.'

You are Al Capone today. A nurse is restraining you, calls for more help. You are throwing punches and the more you throw, the more we try and block them, banking you up in a wall of pillows.

'Get out of my fucking way.'

Your accent has never been so good. Pure *Boardwalk Empire*. I make mental note. I can feel a whole world of parts for you opening up. As you are swinging punches, I see your eyes track my face, you are desperate not to hurt me, hurt anyone. There are four nurses now trying to hold you down. I step outside. I can hear your screaming no matter how far I walk along the corridor. This is frightening. This is so fucking frightening. I tell myself I need to get new glasses. The edge of reality is becoming blurred. Quite literally, there's a fuzz, bleaching out the corners of my vision. I think it might be the radiators pumping out heat, drying up the air, cracking the paint on the metal of the radiator knobs that I persistently try and fail to turn down. That burn your fingers like a motherfucker.

I have taken to swearing a lot. In solidarity with Jacob, perhaps?

Fuck . . . Fuck . . . fucking . . . fuckity . . . fuck . . .

I am so fucking frightened.

I find myself wiping away fat tears, snorting back snot between gulping jagged breaths, perched in the hospital toilet cubicles, knowing that there is someone waiting outside, wanting to come in, but this is the only place I can get any peace, any quiet, any still. Where I am not observed, as I anxiously try and keep my shit together for the children. Where I can get away from your increasingly, terrifying shapeshifting, as you mentally hurl yourself between alternating fractured states.

'Get out of my fucking way . . . Fuck . . . Fuck . . . Fuck . . .'

Rabbis, terrorists, ageing depressed salesmen, but never crazy lunatics.

You are too convincing, too good in this role.

And then as quick, you are calm again, the storm momentarily past, your right hand idly smoothing out the sheet you have been clutching as you turn your face to the wall.

We are waiting for an ambulance. It is going to take you to the intensive therapy unit at the National Hospital in Queen Square. It's ten minutes from UCH, one of the best neurology departments in the world and your MS consultant, Dr C, feels it is the best place. They are concerned. All tests are coming back normal. After the last MRI, after you nearly died, the results come back. Your brain is fine. There is no obvious swelling. The lesions are the same as they were three months before, when they did your twice-yearly check. They don't know what is wrong with you. They still don't know what is wrong with you. But you are getting worse.

We are all tired, exhausted. I am crying, pressing my forehead against the peeling plaster, somewhere far away from you. I have called your best friend, Mattie. You're godfather to his son, Isaac. I speak to Eliza, his wife, a good friend, a friend who will be there throughout.

'I don't think he is going to make it, Eliza.'

I am standing in the lift lobby on the fourth floor of UCH, waiting for the doors to open and close, my face, like Jacob's, turns to the wall, my cellphone to my ear, craving some kind of privacy. The words I say are intimate.

'I don't think he is going to make it . . .'

Finally, an ambulance arrives, Josh travels with you. Your mum, dad and Deb follow in the car. I go home. I need to see the children. It is very late.

'Insane . . . insane . . .' You are restless and shouting, all the way.

'. . . INSANE . . . INSANE . . .'

Later, I think Deb tells me that as you arrived at Queen Square, and they were wheeling you out of the ambulance, you shouted,

'Rape . . . rape—'

But when I ask her, months later, she has no record of this, no memory. I have imagined it, imagined this is what you

shouted as you're on your rocket hurtling into an abyss.
My mind, like yours, is spinning out of control, lost in a
black hole.

Once you are sedated and in your new bed, you are
clearly relieved to see Josh and Deb.

'Surprising . . . ridiculous . . . so surprising.'
They are not sure if you mean to be here or to see them.
But they reassure you.

'Goodnight, Jake. You are in the right place.'
And you are. At last, you are in the right place.
Far from home. Beyond anything you have experienced
before.
Out in space.
I realise I have forgotten my sister's birthday.

A red-brick building, the National Hospital for Neurology
and Neurosurgery, faces the garden in Queen Square, throbbing with tourists and patients and students. It was founded
in 1859, the first hospital to be established in England
dedicated exclusively to treating the diseases of the nervous
system. There's a mobile MRI truck parked close by and
the clang of magnets is audible as you pass, letting you
know another patient is being scanned. Uber drivers park
where they shouldn't and irritate ambulance drivers,
waiting to pick up patients newly released. In one corner
of the square, there is a fig tree, already scattering fruit
over car bonnets and pavement, making passers-by skid.
An urban oasis, the drone of traffic along Southampton
Row, with its tourist shops and knocking-shop hotels, a
distant hum that underscores the birdsong.

When I walk along the corridor the following day, I sanitise my hands at every stop. The level of care in MITU is obvious. The nurses are a different breed to any we have met before; they move quietly, tenderly around the patients, who are all struggling with different kinds of brain disease and injury. The entire unit is being moved down imminently to a brand-new converted ward on the ground floor. I feel hopeful. The smell of new paint always makes me feel hopeful.

Opposite you is a young man, no more than thirty. He is sitting up in a wheelchair, dribbling, trying to focus on the threads of the blanket that are covering his legs. I will later learn his name is Amir. Attached to him are the wires and tubes of ventilators and oxygen tanks and blood pressure gauges that generate the cacophony of bleeps and high-pitched alarms, that reassure the nurses that the patients are breathing, and alert them when they're not. When he turns, I see he only has half a head. There is a gap where the left side of his brain should be. And over the gap, roughly taped, a piece of greasy-looking medical paper, on which someone has scrawled in thick black felt tip 'DO NOT REMOVE THIS FLAP'. I cannot see how he is still alive. Yet his eyes idly follow me from time to time, his head cocked. When visitors come to see Amir I hear the voices of other friends and relatives lovingly talking to him. Despite the fact he neither speaks nor can focus, an iPad is held up for him to see their faces.

They have started you on a five-day course of steroids. You drift in and out of consciousness. Your mum comes in to visit, and you are suddenly alert. You have been to this hospital. You come every month for the injection that

41

manages your MS. The injection that was suddenly withdrawn in the March before you collapsed. The injection that we don't know yet has caused your collapse. That has caused the collapse of 21 other people across the world. Twelve whilst on the wonder drug. And 9 in the months following withdrawal from the drug. But we don't know yet that you are possibly number 22 and the only UK case that we know of.

'I've been here loads of times, Mum.'
You fall asleep again. But wake up again when your sister comes in.

'Hey Tash. How are you doing? It's great to see you. How's Luke?'
Then you drift to sleep again. Only now you are clenching your fists, your eyes are glazed, and you have started to do this strange thing of sucking in your bottom lip, that makes your top lip and teeth stick out. Like you are attempting a bad impersonation of Freddie Mercury. The muscles of your cheeks twitch.

You move through different stages.
Deb, brilliant Deb, my lovely sister-in-law, records them, when I can't be there.
Asleep
Calm
Lucid
Muddled
Agitated
Uncomfortable
Sedated
Glazed
Vacant

You are fascinating. Terrifying and fascinating. You are my favourite subject. My only subject. I Google every tick. Every grimace. Searching for what is wrong. I am an expert. Every day there is a new theory.

I am monstrous. I am increasingly monstrous. Territorial. So territorial I shock myself. The feeling that I am losing you is compounded by the sense that you are held somehow, someway by the collective. At times it is unbearable. I have a profound sense of being shut out. Politely we side-step one another, your family who visit day and night. Your parents, brother, sister, playing relay, checking in and checking out, quietly passing the baton with a word or a smile.

June is tipping into July and still there are no answers. Words come less frequently now. You are growing more and more silent. But when they do, we grip them, blowing off the dust like archaeologists trying to piece together how they fit. And the almost imperceptible ticks have started, your fingers rippling against the sheets, hands resting by your side. Propped up with pillows, you sit up, increasingly absorbed in some silent, invisible pursuit, lost somewhere deep in your head. The flicker of reaction moves quietly across your face. You raise a brow, curl your top lip, and all the time the fingers tap, tap, tap, as if keeping time to some silent concerto that only you can hear.

I try and juggle my other life, my working life. An American studio executive is in town and asks if we can meet at her hotel. She is over for a few days and wants an update on a rewrite of a studio movie, a dark psychological female serial killer thriller I am midway through. Weirdly, it is light relief, to go home at night and work out the mechanics of how said female serial killer will asphyxiate the mother she hates, during a prison visit. So dutifully, I brush my hair and put myself back together for the day. But when I arrive at her hotel, the American studio executive is shaking with jetlag and needs to eat, and I am giddy and blurry eyed. It is not a good combination, and halfway through the meeting I realise I am neither of sane mind nor inclined to make light chat. The hotel restaurant we have decamped to is too loud, too filled with chattering tourists, the world too oblivious to the nightmare I now inhabit. Less than five minutes' walk from here, the protagonist in that other life, that life that once was ours, mine, is lost mid-scene. I make my excuses and leave.

On my return I pass Dr K, one of your consultants. He is smiling, and beautiful and brilliant, and in another life we fall in love. He has something he wants to tell me, delivered with almost eager surprise.

'Anti-NMDA receptor encephalitis. Have you heard of it?' he asks a little too enthusiastically. They have sent off your bloods again as they still can't find any signs of infection. But now they are looking for a tumour, often a trigger for anti-NMDA. We punch the air, hoping it is cancer. What world are we in that cancer would be a relief? A positive anti-NMDA receptor encephalitis diagnosis would be a win. I can feel hope daring to return. It's rare and it causes an inflammation of the brain. It would normally be found in young women. They are testing for it. The results are not immediate. And it seems a long shot. But I can see Dr K is excited. On the scent of something at last.

Jesse and Mabel are desperate to see you. I have kept them at bay for the last few days, worried by how they will react. You are worse. Worse than you have ever been. But they need to see you. Only when we get there, I lose my nerve and persuade Mabel to stay downstairs. To this day I don't know why. I let her sit alone. I don't know if it was in the car or the reception, with its sticky surfaces and cold stone floor, but it is a mis-step that will be imprinted on her long after. Perhaps it was a desire to keep her away from the reality that is catapulting both of them out of childhood into searing painful adult misery. I wanted her to stay fourteen for just a little longer.

When we would tuck them into bed, when they were infants and woke up, fitful and afraid, we would tell them,

'We love you always . . . We're here . . . We're not going anywhere.'

How could we have been so certain?

I turn a phrase over in my head, I don't know who said it.

'Childhood is a promise never kept.'

And we have broken that promise.

I know now that I should have gripped Mabel's hand and stood by her side and let her see, even the worst bits. She deserved this. I will tell her, in a few months' time, that adults make mistakes. I will tell myself it was because she had a sore throat. And that you are not you, but I will regret this decision. One of my biggest regrets.

She, perhaps more than anyone, needed to see you.

We may not have favourite children, but they can have a favourite parent.

Jacob was hers.

The joy of children is the magical game of tracing back the traits of shared DNA. Jacob's absolute earthed, direct, honest, open-hearted warmth is woven deep into Mabel's blood. She has inherited Jacob's spirit of adventure. She's the first to jump, to push herself down a hill, always cheered on by her father, inspired by his love of play. She has an ability to be carefree, to dance and enjoy the company of others, yet all the while quietly sketching and observing and listening, another skill honed and worked on in his company. Their relationship has always been close, unique.

I have a myriad of photos of Jacob adventuring with his children. There was frequently a call and change of plan, as he reconfigured their days, usually when I was working or immersed in a script or shoot, home late. A few months before his collapse, there was a spontaneous trip to Amsterdam, decided upon on a cold March morning because the canals had frozen over. It was a once-in-a-hundred-years event, so why not pick them up after school on a Friday afternoon and be there by evening? There's a picture of Jacob and Mabel taken during the week they drove around Naples, perched side by side on a rooftop eating pizza, a shimmering bay beyond, laughing. A summer both children spent interrailing with their father, the photos from Paris, Berlin, Split, wherever they had landed, popping up at regular intervals on my phone: wet from thunderstorms or eating the best hot dogs in Berlin. Or a momentary piece of iPhone footage of an ethereal ectoplasm jellyfish, caught through grainy light, their muffled watery conversation just audible underneath.

I will tell myself in the years to come at least they have this . . . had this.

More than most get in a lifetime, these memories.

And what's remembered, lives.
What's—
. . . Remembered—
. . . Lives.

You are sleepy when Jesse arrives. He holds your hand. You don't acknowledge him. You are sleeping more and more. We go home with Josh. Huw, my younger brother, and his wife, Sophie, are cooking us lunch. My mum is sitting in the garden, drinking wine. It's the weekend and she has a day off; ironically, she is in an Alan Bennett play set in a hospital. She's rallying, as she does, amusing us with funny stories of cast and show. Dorcas, my ever-present sister, has filled the house with flowers. We eat delicious roast chicken and salad under an umbrella. Later, Josh and Jesse watch football on the TV, the World Cup building to its final stages.

I need to say something about football. What football means to Jacob. To us. As a family. I was brought up largely by my mother. Not that she couldn't have been a fan. But traditionally football is something passed down by father to son. And football didn't feature in our childhoods. Bernard, Jacob's father, passed on many things including a love of cured meat and Sondheim musicals, and a warmth and generosity that fills a room. Jacob found football on his own. He is an ardent Spurs fan, a passion now shared with his son and daughter. We've had season tickets since before Jesse was born.

At first, I used to hate the cold weekends and evenings spent at games. But I've come to see that what Jacob gave

Jesse and Mabel was currency. In any town, in any country, any new school, football will find you friends. A connection. A link. Whatever team you support. Josh is ardent Arsenal. On opposing match days the brothers never speak. Still, it bonds them. And when Jesse, a few years on from his father's collapse, arrives at Edinburgh University to study neuroscience amidst a global pandemic, it will be football that will save him. Football that will break the rule of six.

And it will be football that will start to bring Jacob back. After this has happened. After this too has passed. This hell we are about to spiral further into, the small stones we will throw into the pool of water that Jacob's brain will become, that will send ripples back to the surface. That will tell us he is somewhere. In there. Deep down on the ocean bed. It will be football that will finally make him hear. Make him listen.

We are exhausted. This is exhausting.

The days blur as we watch you, slipping in and out of lucidity, as if you are shutting down, your breathing growing more and more shallow by the day. Two weeks since your collapse, and they still do not know how to fix this. You have a growing team of consultants, specialists in seizure, epilepsy, immunology, neurology, infectious diseases, MS. Teams and teams of men and women, doctors and nurses, drawing blood and draining spinal fluid and gathering in hushed consultation around your bed and in corners of corridors, whispering, concern and puzzlement written on their faces, quickly covered with a smile or a professional nod of the head when we pass. There are high-tech IT bods who attach wires through a mesh cap to your brain, the jagged graphs on the screen by your bed monitoring the now hourly seizures. Now we know the flickering fingers and lip-smacking were an early sign that these were to come. Keisha, your nurse, beautiful with dark cornrows and a dry wit, tells us you remembered your name and birthdate today, hopeful amidst the daily blurring of your mind, words coming like echoes from a deep cave now, sporadic, but still just audible if you stay alert, listen.

'Can you tell us your name?'

'Jacob.'

'Can you tell us your birthdate?'

'22.07.72.'

'Do you know where you are?'

'No.'

Your dad texts me that you gave Dr C a thumbs up this evening. I read it standing in Londis on the corner of our road and cry. These sea changes, turns in the current, come as quick as they go, until we are all caught in the same soporific state as you are, unable to give answers to those questions the kind and concerned ask us.

'No . . . they don't know what's wrong with him yet?'

'It's difficult to describe . . . he's awake but he's not awake . . . he's changed . . . he's changing.'

One day I go in and you are sitting up as the nurses hover around you, taking blood and trying to wash you. Today when you see me, you hold your arms out wide, in an almost flamboyant gesture, lucid, when yesterday you were mute and withdrawn. These are the schizophrenic changes, the bursts of light through the clouds, the low-level shape-shifting, that bemuse and blind us, the visitors.

'You are so kind. You are so caring. You are so loving,' you say.

The nurses smile at me delighted as the compliments fall. And I am both moved and alarmed. Moved, because I so wish I had cared for you in the way you wanted, so wish I had been more kind and loving when so often I was less than all of these things. Alarmed, because flattering as this is, this is not you anymore. The tumble of words, their gushing nature, the way you look to the nurses, checking your audience is entertained, confirms you have left the room. Surprising for an actor, I know, but you were never one to take the limelight, preferring to laugh rather than be the laughter, to be charmed rather than charming, to listen rather than be the focus of attention in the room.

The lip-smacking has got worse, and I bring Carmex and smear thick cream on your skin. You pucker them and then won't speak to me for two days. When you do, you're now playing an eager host, sitting in your bed, introducing the nurses like they are much-loved dinner guests that you don't entirely know.

'This is Lisa . . .'

It's not.

'Penny.'

You correct yourself, your eyes tracking her name badge, embarrassed that you've got it wrong.

'This is Abi . . . my lovely whiff . . . wiffey . . . wifey . . . wife.'

You fall asleep that night talking about football to Josh.

Then suddenly wake saying— 'We need to script this. Script this.'

Josh asks you if you know who he is.

'You're my brother,' you reply.

Then Dr C points to Jesse.

'Who is this?'

'My gorgeous, beautiful boy,' you offer proudly.

And you pull Jesse in for a kiss, through a tangle of wires, smacking your lips, animated, hugging him.

We have a result. Dr K is pleased with himself. He is right. Anti-NMDA receptor encephalitis. Strongly positive, found in your spinal fluid, post your lumbar puncture. This is the game changer. This is the answer we have been waiting for. Now they can throw everything at it; placing a plasma exchange machine by your bed that for five days will strip the blood of plasma, the straw-colour fluid that contains all the red and white blood cells, platelets, protein and nutrients. They will take the old plasma to test, and replace it with a fluid known as Octaplas as they try to clean your body of the rogue antibodies that continue to inflame your brain. They give you extra seizure medications and courses of steroids and immunosuppressant drugs. You are going to be alright.

You are going to be alright.

And I want to believe this.

I want this to be true.

But somewhere nagging, tugging at hope, at optimism, is a growing sense that it is never going to be OK again.

I Google for so long that my computer dies. While I'm

rifling around the house in search of a laptop lead I see the garden is filled with foxes in the early morning light.

I stare at them and they stare back, with such swagger that at one point the larger in the pack comes right up to the kitchen window, pressing his nose against the glass. So close and so bold that not even Styler's crazed scraping of greasy paws against the kitchen walls scares him away.

We retreat to the bed, listening to the foxes' claws scratching against the roof lining of the shed. I clench Styler's mouth, like we are in some comedy caper, trying to stop him from howling. I am almost proud of his desire not to give up, not to give in. To let the scavenging foxes know that, though his owners are cowed, depleted, destroyed, there is still a fighting spirit living somewhere in here.

This is what Wikipedia says:

Anti-NMDA receptor encephalitis is a type of <u>brain inflammation</u> due to <u>antibodies</u>.[4] Early symptoms may include <u>fever</u>, headache, and feeling tired.[1][2] This is then typically followed by <u>psychosis</u> which presents with <u>false beliefs</u> (delusions) and <u>seeing or hearing things that others do not see or hear</u> (hallucinations).[1] People are also often agitated or confused.[1] Over time <u>seizures</u>, <u>decreased breathing</u>, and <u>blood pressure and heart rate variability</u> typically occur.[]

About half of cases are associated with <u>tumours</u>, most commonly <u>teratomas</u> of the <u>ovaries</u>.[1][4] Another established trigger is <u>herpesviral encephalitis</u>, while the cause in others cases is unclear.[1][4][5] The underlying mechanism is <u>auto-immune</u> with the primary target the <u>GluN1</u> <u>subunit</u> of the

N-methyl D-aspartate receptors (NMDAR) in the brain.[1][6] Diagnosis is typically based on finding specific antibodies in the cerebral spinal fluid.[1] MRI of the brain is often normal.[2] Misdiagnosis is common.[6]

Treatment is typically with immunosuppressive medication and, if a tumour is present, surgery to remove it.[1] With treatment about 80% of people have a good outcome.[1] Outcomes are better if treatment is begun earlier.[2] Long term mental or behavioural problems may remain.[2] About 4% of those affected die from the condition.[2] Recurrence occurs in about 10% of people.

Long term mental or behavioural problems may remain.

I read this line several times.

About 4% of those affected die from the condition.

I stop Googling.

I want to be excited.

I play along.

But Dr C errs on the side of caution too.

'We're not out of the woods. We're still in the woods,' says Dr C.

It is something I will hear him say a lot.

For a long time.

And it is true. You are struggling. Your body is struggling to manage the NMDA neurons attacking themselves in your head. Your heart rate is fluctuating, blood pressure dangerously rises and falls, and your breathing continues to grow shallower by the day. You had more seizures last night. You are sleepy and benign. Drugged up. Drifting away. You mumble so quietly we have to lean in close.

On the final day, what I now see as the final day when

there was still some semblance of you here, Jesse sits by your bed and I hear you tell him,

'In a perfect world we'd all get on. In a perfect world there'd be no cancer. In a perfect world we'd all love one another. In a perfect world . . .'

I realise only later that no one has told you that there are no tumours. No cancer. The early search for malignancy long called off. I realise you think you have cancer. Anti-NMDA receptor encephalitis. It should have been triggered by a tumour. But you have no tumours. You have anti-NMDA receptor encephalitis. I keep saying it. Keep repeating it to people who ask, frightened I will forget the name. The one person I didn't tell was you.

You have been in hospital sixteen days now and whilst you keep on breathing, I am out of puff. I visit my therapist who has come off her maternity leave early to see me. The days of hurtling through rush hour traffic in the daily back and forth to the hospital, feeding and running the kids around whilst trying to meet deadlines and get scripts out, late-night Googling and insomnia is rapidly taking its toll. And, of course, I would have a therapist. Of course, I would be this much of a cliché. But I am so grateful. I am a ball of rage by the time I knock on her door. My knuckles ache because at night I scrunch my hands so tight that by morning I have the red imprint of clenched fingers marked on my chest. In here, in this room, the fury that threatens to suffocate me and drain the room of every last breath of oxygen, spills like milk brought to the boil. I want to blame someone, anyone. I want to know how to get out of this fix. This corner that we are trapped in. I want to wake up from this living nightmare. People use that term, but now I understand it – it is surreal, this feeling that my life, my other life, is happening somewhere else, and somehow the day to day has drifted far away.

I let rip for five minutes and she is kind, she listens, she is part of the jigsaw that will get me through this. Then there's a call. It is your mum and Tash, and two consultants, also on the line. They have been visiting you and you have deteriorated. They need to intubate you and put you on a ventilator. Once they do that you won't be able to speak anymore.

You won't be able to— . . . speak—

. . . anymore.

I leave my therapist and drive to the hospital. I have to talk to you. I need to talk to you. I realise that I promised Mabel she would see you, she would speak to you again. I promised her this on the days I have told her to stay home. I don't know what to do. I think of calling the school, getting someone to bring them both in. Because you can't stay much longer, frazzled from all the electrical activity, and your brain is tired and your lungs are out of puff, but when I arrive and see you, I know at once this is irrelevant.

You need some peace, some rest.

And it's only a courtesy that they've called me.

They don't need my consent.

'I love you Jacob,' I say as you drift off into your milky drug-induced coma.

'. . . Deeply . . . Deeply,' you whisper back.

These are the last words you will say.

It is the end of June.

You will not speak again until January.

January, six months of an aching, at times unbearable, silence.

And you will never be the same.

3

It is a Saturday morning, in February. Four months before what happened, happens. We're sleeping in late, the blinds down.

'I had the weirdest dream last night . . .'
It is unusual for me to remember my dreams, and if I'm honest I want to eat my own eyeballs when people try to tell me theirs. Recounted as if you are being given their most prized motorway route, every detail delivered as if somehow it will miraculously cut your journey time down. And I can't tell them I don't care, it's just the brain doing a spot of filing. Except the dreams of my children. I love the dreams of my children, suspecting that somewhere within the chaotic jumble of their night-time thoughts, I will get to see the inner workings of their minds, formulating theories that reveal what they are feeling and not saying. Theories that I will share with you, often when they have gone to bed. But now it is Saturday and you and I are lazy and for once it is our own dreams that we idly trade, drifting in and out of that sweet spot where you want longer to sleep, but keep catching on aimless, fragmented conversation.
So, this is how mine went—
'I'm looking out of the window. We are in our old bedroom downstairs, staring out of the bay window, and

I can see dark-clothed men, swathed in black scarves and holding Kalashnikovs. They are clambering out of cars and systematically going in and out of the houses of our neighbours. It is silent, but they move like black ink along the street, coming closer, and I know soon they are coming for us.'

Silence.

I think you've gone back to sleep.

But you've not.

You've moved onto your own.

'I think I'm lying in a bed, it's some kind of bed, but it's not my own and everyone is around me, looking at me, and I can't speak. I can't move.'

And you turn and look at me.

'. . . It was horrible.'

You have sleep caught in your eyelashes and before I can tell you you have caught my eye infection and you really must use that cream by the sink, you are up and in the shower.

'We must stop eating so late,' I shout.

But I don't think you hear.

They have moved you downstairs into the new MITU-intensive care ward. We have to be buzzed in through two separate doors to get into the ward. Between the two doors, there is a cramped reception where we can sit and watch TV. On first sight, it is a little like staying in the lobby of a budget hotel, and for a moment I hope there might be a mini bar. But there's not. Only wipe-clean plastic and strange rubberised chair fabric. Clean and perfectly adequate, but with no frills, designed for people to pass through. No one is expected to stay long. But we do. As the days pass, this square of lino will ebb and flow with people like us, anxious relatives, clutching Starbucks coffee, going cold in our hands as we try to catch a passing consultant, or make it through the opening doors to the MITU ward before they electronically snap shut. And always underscored by the relentlessly dramatic voices of day-time TV while we are stuck in our own never-ending *Truman Show*.

Occasionally a nurse will turn the TV off, and I don't know what's worse. The bright chat or the uncomfortable silence, punctured by the painful exchanges, the swapping of updates between us, the visitors, about those we love, the visited. We are divided into those who like to chat and those who avoid eye contact. I learn to read the signals, know when bad news has been delivered, or hope has been ignited. And then they are gone, never to be seen again. I start to count the days, taking quiet pride as the figure goes up.

'Still here . . . still here.'

A quiet, ticking mantra that accompanies me as I park my car, hurrying in again.

There are five beds on the ward. Three facing the main desk where the nurses sit. And then two side rooms. One to the right. And one to the left. You are in the one to the right. It has a glass wall, so they can always watch you. The nurses, the brilliant nurses, who turn you and brush your teeth and check your stats and infuse you with meds. And all the while you sleep. A restless Sleeping Beauty. Your room is futuristic, and you lie, wired up to screens and monitors, with the EEG mesh cap once more stuck to your scalp. They tell me they had to use the bag on you again last night. You are fighting the ventilator, not breathing with the machine, biting on your tube. In a minute, the anaesthetist is coming down to give you a tracheotomy. I wonder where they will cut you. You are the strongest man I know but the one area you are squeamish about is around your Adam's apple. I want reassurances that they won't cut you here.

Dr S, the nice registrar, reassures me the level of sedation you are under is like an operation state, and you won't feel a thing. They keep playing around with your sedation, trying to quell the seizure activity that leaves you twitching and repetitively blinking. Dr S tells us that they treated a woman in a very similar condition to you last year, and now she is home with her child. We grab at these straws. I ask them if they can do it without shaving too much of your beard. And if they could miss your Adam's apple, please.

They are feeding you through a tube in your nose, and you are losing weight. That's one way to do it, I think. The months working out at the gym, always doing battle with your love of food. The sit-ups, press-ups, knee lifts, the pay-off for your Saturday lunch runs to Salvino's, the best deli this side of the Euston Road, where you would regularly go to purchase slabs of parmesan and thinly sliced salamis to be consumed throughout the week. When I think of you, it is always with the fridge door open, in search of a snack, even if dinner is minutes away.

You were never thin, but now you are positively bird-like. The bed tilted upright, your legs splayed and raised, your head turned a little to the side. You lie, pinned like a specimen in a lab. They have put padded mesh boxing gloves on your hands, to stop you pulling at your wires when you occasionally stir. Funny, I remember you telling me stories of your trainer Louis, holding up pads that you would lamely punch in the gym. Your tongue moves a little from time to time when we talk to you, as if you are trying to formulate words in a language you no longer speak. Your temperature keeps spiking and you are drenched in sweat. You have developed a chest infection and your liver is not working as well as it should. But we will come to see that this is all part of being long term in an intensive care unit. The fluctuating rise and fall of pneumonia. The infections in your IV lines that come and go, the days your kidneys are failing and your liver is tiring, the nights when we are not sure if you will live.

It's not like this in the movies.

In the movie, you lie quietly, serenely.

In the movie, no one tells you how busy the industry around a coma is.

Physios come and pummel your chest, to remove the gunk that is gathering in your lungs, and the nurses rush around you, as your care is cranked up. A changing carousel of brilliant men and women; Richie, gentle, with ornate tattoos inked on both arms. Jenny, intimidating at first, but quickly revealed as a warm New Zealander, in charge, on rotation with Stuart, or Shakespeare Cam as we call him, such is his resemblance to Cam on *Modern Family*, with the addition of a Shakespearean beard. Maricel, always smiling, quietly working around us, all reading to you, playing you music and stroking your arm. Beatrice, calm and earnest, who exchanges stories of Seville with Jesse who is studying Spanish for A-level. Many of them far from home, yet diligent, like worker bees, focused on keeping you alive, caring for you like they would family.

We are holding our nerve, trusting you will get through another infection, your temperature spiking again and again, you are overheating, fever taking hold of your body once more. Swabs are taken and Penny, Jenny's Kiwi compatriot, with a pink streak in her fringe and a dry wit, confirms you have tested positive for E. coli. On bad days they cover you with a blanket pumped with ice water, trying to bring your temperature down, trying to control the maelstrom in your brain. The mesh EEG cap, that makes you look part factory worker, part like Pinhead in *Hellraiser*, is put on, then taken off again, as they try to give the skin on your scalp a break every seven days. I watch the jagged lines of your brain activity on the monitor at the end of your bed, trying and failing to decipher what the ever-changing graph means. I learn that the sharp consistent peaks are seizures, which I report on as I cross paths with your mum, dad, Tash, Josh and Deb, like bleary-eyed, sleep-deprived shift workers clocking in and out.

Through the glass wall of your room, a young Polish man in his early twenties lies in the next bed. He is being fed by his mother, Violetta. She has been here five months, since her son collapsed with what looked like a cold. He is paralysed from the neck down. I never ascertain exactly why. Sweet and watchful, her English, like my Polish, is non-existent. We smile at one another and later I learn she is staying with her son's flatmates, friends he has made whilst working in a bar over here. One day I come and she has gone back to Poland, taking her son with her so he can recover in a hospital closer to home.

The aptly named Belle, petite in her late teens and smiling like a Disney princess, takes the Polish boy's bed. She lies for months recovering from some unknown illness that has left her bed-bound. Every day, her mum and sister perch on her bed, their bright chatter momentarily lifting the spirits on the ward. While one lovingly combs her long blonde hair the other turns the pages of a magazine for her, cooing over the latest celebrity gossip. On Saturdays, her boyfriend travels up by train, and I can hear them talking, whispering and giggling behind the curtain, watching TV together on an iPad, trying to kill time. One day, word goes round that they are prepping Belle to go to rehab upstairs. The next day she is gone and we quietly mourn her absence, the set around us once more shifting again. No doubt a card from Belle's family, thanking the staff for saving her life, will be added to the notice board of letters and photos pinned up by the entrance. On good days, inspiring. On bad, these photos and letters taunt us, so impossible it seems, the ask to bring you back.

There is a vigil for a young actor, his family pacing in the waiting room, his sweet girlfriend a constant, as it becomes apparent that the young man is going to die. It crosses my mind that in a ward of only five beds, the odds of finding two thespians in one hospital seem slim. But then I am reminded we are in London. The young actor was touring only a few weeks before, in *Grease*. Or is it

Dirty Dancing? The outpourings on Facebook later confirm he is much loved, a talented young star, cut short in his prime. The infection that has felled him came on quickly. The shock is etched on his mother's face. Jesse and I go and buy them Starbucks, handing over the tray of hot chocolates and biscuits in quiet solidarity, a feeble offering in the face of such tragedy and pain. And then they are gone and a new patient arrives, another miraculous sleight of hand. Now there's a new cast playing and the surreal nature of the experience hits us again and makes me feel like I'm in some strange site-specific Punch Drunk production. The consultants change as swiftly as the patients do, their tenure never longer than three months, the brief intimacies lost as another consultant rotates to another ward, and we must adjust again. I am told by another doctor friend that this is deliberate, designed to stop anyone becoming too attached.

Your dad is reading Arnold Wesker's biography to you. It was Wesker who said the playwright is director in the stage directions. It is the same when writing a screenplay. It is in the action between the dialogue that the writer can direct the eye of the audience. Or so we like to believe. Early in my career, in one of my first TV shows, a director sat me down and told me,

'You have six images on this page. I can only shoot two, so work out which ones are important.'

I have spent my life looking at the world through this lens, working out what to keep and what I should throw away. In my mind, I cast this play, watching the changing characters like a magpie, storing anecdote and detail in my head. Only we are all bad actors, not up to speed with our lines, not quite sure of our parts. In the past, on feverish nights, when I am late on a deadline and have set myself an impossible task, working into the early hours to finish a script, I dream in scenes and mentally edit conversation around me, the writer in me bleeding into the everyday. Quietly, discreetly, mentally, I correct a word or cut a line of dialogue in conversation. It can be something innocuous that my children have said over dinner. I can forget that this is real life, not to be curated, tampered with. Yet still, if the rhythm is out during the most innocuous exchanges, I will mentally rearrange the words, rework how it should have been said.

The Amazon delivery driver, when my neighbour is out:
'I was going to leave this at No. 19, but they're not in. Alright if I take a photo by your door please?'
Too long, something snappier, trust the image will deliver the intention.
'No. 19 not in. Alright if I take a photo?'
Better.
It's a distracting hypervigilance that can pull me out of any normal human interaction, leave me scattered. When my daughter was a baby, she used to reach her hand up, turn my face to look at her, such was my distraction, even when feeding her in the middle of the night. It's a state that can still wake me, make me sit bolt upright, speak the character's lines out loud, always trying to improve them.
Do better.
Madness, flaring, like eczema.
On those nights, you would say,
'Slow down. You're going to miss your life.'

And you were right.

I once wept, on a perfect night, with you, after a delicious supper, overlooking a beautiful bay, somewhere exotic. Because it was too perfect, because happiness was too unsettling, because the imperfect is my natural state, the place that truly fascinates.

But to live it every day?

It's exhausting.

Amir, the young man who was here when you first arrived, is making progress. One day his brother stops me and reassures me Amir was just like you at the start. I am both grateful and alarmed. Amir is going up to rehab soon. Yet his head still painfully lolls to the side, and he dribbles. No one can tell me how you will be. I cry to my sister, calling her from my car on the endless zigzag home, Russell Square, Bloomsbury to Amwell Street, Amwell to Liverpool Road, hitting Holloway and up to Hornsey. She listens and consoles me as I drive and weep.

On one of my crazed late-night Google trawls I read up about the immune modifier drug Jacob came off in March, part of a MS drug trial he was on. I find a European medical report and learn that others have got sick as a result of taking the same medication. There are cases of brain inflammation, and in one patient the same anti-NMDA receptor encephalitis that Jacob is now battling. When I bring my latest theory to Dr C's attention, he reassures me, there are great minds working on getting you better, he promises me he is reviewing the evidence, but that the reports all say you felt you were doing well on the drug at the time. And you were, the headaches and the lethargy were, we told ourselves, the pay-off for keeping the worse symptoms of your MS at bay. I want to believe Dr C, but as he puts down the phone, his parting shot is,

'We are still in the woods.'

The woods?

I dream of black holes, of hurtling dark endless space. I'm irritated by this interruption, this mix of metaphors, tampering with my own creative interpretation of events, internally I'm correcting, editing again, mentally filing this conversation away.

One day Jesse and I are walking down the street when he points at something. A poster, slap bang opposite a favourite tapas bar. The slice of traffic momentarily blocking the view. We cross, quietly marvelling at how apt it is, both choked up and hugging one another. A black poster, with white lettering that simply reads:

I am just resting my eyes.

Dad.

If you look there are signs everywhere.

In December, a few months later, I will track down the artist who randomly fly-posts across London and he will kindly send me a print, free of charge, and I will frame it and give it to Jesse.

Jesse.

Our beautiful boy.

Jesse Ira Krichefski.

The seed that we planted, that sowed you and I together, conceived only a few months after we met, discovered in a hotel room in Toronto. I'm there working on the early genesis of a play, along with a contingent of other writers and directors from the UK. At first, I think I must be ill – it is unlike me to hole up in my room, eating endless room service whilst the others go out and play. And then one day, as I step out of the shower, I catch my reflection in the mirror and I see something about my body is different. I buy three pregnancy tests and the third try, the stick shaking in my hand, confirms what I already know. I give little away to you on the phone, complain I am not feeling well. And then cry on the plane all the way home. I'm not entirely sure why, just that it all felt so over-whelming. But then you surprise me at the airport, waiting with open arms and smiling as I tearily reveal what you have already suspected.

I am pregnant.

'Isn't it fantastic?' you will say.

And it is.

Fantastic.

Jesse, because we both love it. The Roberta Flack song is going to be played on a loop when you are born but is forgotten in the rush and hue of a grim birthing suite of a North Middlesex hospital.

Ira after Gershwin. Though we both agree Sondheim is king, Stephen doesn't work as well with Jesse.

And then the discussion over whether he should carry my last name, quickly kiboshed because anyone with Morgan Krichefski as a last name sounds like a firm of solicitors. Later we will discover Jesse in Hebrew means 'gift'.

Our swift gift.

Born almost a year after our first date when Jacob cooked a terrible curry, in a house he was looking after for a friend.

We ended up watching a very earnest TV show, featuring Daniel Craig pre-Bond. I remember nothing of the programme, except the sense of Jacob nervously hovering, working out how to make his move. What I do remember is that when it happened, I knew instantly that this was 'him'.

Everything came quickly into my life with Jacob. We collided with absolute velocity. Yet not without the odd bump in the road. On our second date I had to talk him down on the telephone, lost en route to dinner at my flat, in some backwater of East London with no taxi in sight. On our third date we got giddy in Soho and wandered aimlessly for hours, not quite sure how to get home. By our fifth he had virtually moved in.

An actor. I promised myself not an actor. But then the people I have loved the most have been actors at one time or another. My mother, father, sister, brother-in-law, best friends, male and female, all actors, past and present. Since childhood, there has been something about actors I have always loved. Not just that they are my tribe, familiar to me. It is their energy and ability to be 'on' that has always amazed me. Whether in a roomful of strangers or to an audience of one, they burn bright, amusing and fun. My father was a director, and for years ran theatres up and down the country. Most of the places we lived in were furnished with salvaged props, always on the edge of collapse and not designed for real living. Our homes were filled with the whisper of production, the anticipation building as opening night got closer, particularly if it was a play my mother was also involved in. Invariably the first-night party would continue on at our house, the spill of actors squeezed into our kitchen or sprawling on our crappy sofa. Huw was still a baby but Dorcas and I would watch the highs and lows and crazed antics, the late-night indiscretions between cast and crew all part of a familiar blur. The thump of Bob Dylan and Janis Ian reverberating through floorboards is the sound of my childhood, the way I was lulled to sleep, just as the hum of a milk float signalled the dawn.

It is a world not unfamiliar to Jacob. Later we discovered that our fathers knew one another in their twenties. Mine, now dead, was on secondment from the Royal Shakespeare Company, when he directed Bernard in a play at Cambridge University over forty years ago. A week after Jacob and I first met, I am at a birthday party and end up sitting on a sofa, next to Bernard, now a TV producer. He has worked with the writer, whose birthday it is.

Kri . . . chef . . . ski.

It is not a name you forget.

Bernard is charming and I will later tell Jacob,

'I fell in love with your father before I fell in love with you.'

Ping . . .

It felt like a further confirmation that we were of the same tribe.

My mother's best friend was a writer. A novelist. When I was twelve and my parents were separating, we spent a particularly magical summer with her and her children in her four-storey house in North London. On Sundays, her ex-husband, Jewish and an actor, would pick up the children and take them for lunch. And in the evenings, she would come down from her room at the top of the house, where she had been writing, and cook supper and talk with my mother, and her children, then teenagers, so cool and impressive to Dorcas, Huw and me. They introduced us to Snoopy and McDonald's and the brilliance of the top deck of Routemaster buses that could take you from Hampstead to the West End for free. There were boyfriends and other partners and it all somehow worked effortlessly. I longed to be part of it, secretly wishing we never had to leave.

Perhaps it was the breakdown of my parents' marriage, against the backdrop of this new, reconfigured, blended family, that made it seem like the perfect life to me, but I think it is no coincidence that thirty years on, when I have children, it is with an actor, who is Jewish. And who I would live with in a four-storey house in North London where I work until the children grow too big and seem to fill the house with teenage laughter and I find an office. Perhaps what seemed random, so fast, so unthought through, had an absolute sense of destination, of destiny.

But still, when I called my mother and told her that we were pregnant, she said—

'Who? Who is pregnant?' with bewildered disbelief.

Fast. Absolute. Life changing.

Was this always how it was going to be with you and me?

Swift.

Gift.

You.

Me.

*

There is one day, one very bad day, when I sit in the square with your mother and we discuss what we will do if you die. You are hovering in that danger zone again, the zone when I can hear the blood pumping in my chest. Your parents are both sensitive, kind, intelligent people, but these conversations are hard. Shiva, in the Jewish culture, happens quickly, within twenty-four hours. But what do we do? How will it work?

'He can be buried with me and his father,' your mother suggests.

This is kind but problematic on many counts. Judith and Bernard, though the best of friends, have been divorced for many years now. And I think Sam, Bernard's husband, might have something to say about it. But it is a relief, to know there is somewhere, somewhere you can be.

A few weeks after they have put you into a coma, I find a birthday card I planned to give you,

'I guess it's time to start deciding if you want to be buried or cremated.'

In recent years, we had argued, playfully at first but with increasing passion, as to what would happen if one or the other of us died.

Traditionally, Jews are buried.

Would we be buried together?

Is that even what I want?

I am claustrophobic and averse to lying in a box. Would you not want to be with me, ashes scattered across the heath near where we had raised our kids and often liked to go to? You were appalled, at the thought that I would be there, haunting every visit.

'Why ruin a good walk?' you replied.
But eventually you buckled.
'I don't care. I won't be there, so do what you want.'
That unbearable lightness of being again.
And yet it is deceptive.
You are driven, Jacob. You are clinging onto life.
The monitors keep peeping.
The oxygen bag rises and falls.
You live.
You keep on living.
You keep fighting for your life.

For the last couple of years, Jesse and Mabel have gone to Wireless – a music festival in Finsbury Park, a ten-minute amble along the Parkland Walk from where we live – and this year is to be no different. The tickets, stuck to your notice board, found the week before. These tickets terrify me. You have shown me the videos, shot on your iPhone, and I know that as the kids hurl themselves into the front of the crowd, you loiter, close by, ready to reach out an arm to save our daughter from the crush of the mosh pit. You're at ease with the anarchic youth and madness, the loud, grinding rap music, the beer cans and burger wraps crushed under foot.

I have taken for granted the luxury of being in a two-parent household, something I had to adjust to in the early years, it was so long since I had lived with both of mine in the same house, and even when they were together I was largely brought up by my mother. Those tickets do more than terrify me. They kick at the dull ache already heavy in my heart, so heavy that there are days I worry I can't conceal its dark, lingering presence. There's a Jacob-shaped hole now in so many of the precarious, tricky situations that I happily avoided, yet could somehow hitch a ride on, when the adventures were retold. Mentally, I trace my way back through the single-parent households I know, marvelling at the many examples of brilliant, ample parenting managed solo. But I do remember one friend, a single parent since the birth of her daughter, telling me,

'On sports days you're cheering on your own.'

This—?

I don't know how to do this.

I long for the days of Latitude, a festival we went to when the kids were small. I'm nostalgic for the moonlit nights of Guy Garvey singing his haunting, rasping tunes in a crowded field near Southwold. When they were little and we could perch them on our shoulders, as we sang along to every track—

Throw those curtains wide . . .

One day like this a year'd see me right.

But now they are bigger, taller, louder. They dwarf me with their long limbs, and my arms never feel wide enough to hold them fully, keep them safe. Because you are not here. Fearless and unafraid. Captain of our ship. Steering them through the teenage years. My role is to be the second-in-command, gripping your hand as you navigate this sea of noise and elbows, spilt beer and grinding sound. But you are sleeping, chest rising and falling, lying hot under an ice blanket, whilst those around you try to cool you down.

From our bedroom I can hear Stormzy, ringing out across Finsbury Park.

You are miles from here, oblivious to the sound.

And I miss you.

I miss you so much.

It makes me sick I miss you so much.

Josh takes the children to Wireless and Deb takes me to Highgate ponds. After we've queued awkwardly in our bathing costumes, we swim round and round in ordered rotation, passed only by the occasional moorhen or robust swimmer. I bump into someone I was at college with who I haven't seen for years. We tread water while she tells me about her life, barely drawing breath until my fingers are going blue.

'And how are you? ' she eventually asks.

I don't know what to say—

'Jacob is in a coma . . .'

'I think I'm losing my mind . . .'

'Yesterday I thought about killing myself.'

It happened as I was driving in the second-hand, silver Mini Cooper that Jacob surprised me with on my last birthday. I am at traffic lights, staring up at the clock in Kings Cross, returning from another visit to the hospital. And it occurs to me that if I keep driving there is a bridge at Highgate I could jump off. It's a calm thought. The possibility hangs like a warm bath. It shocks me, how soothing the thought is, what comfort it gives me. I had assumed suicide would feel sharper, angrier, more of a tussle.

But then the lights change.

And I drive on, overwhelmed with guilt that I could even think about doing this to my kids, to my family. And yet there is a flicker of curiosity as to what it will mean, how the world will react, if I say,

'. . . By the traffic lights at Kings Cross. I thought of doing it then. It was that or watch another episode of *Grey's Anatomy?*'

But I don't say any of this to her, the old college friend I have just met, who is now treading water, smiling blankly at me.

'Good . . . All good . . .'

I swim on, relieved that the consequences of such a dramatic confession have been narrowly averted. I get out of the pond. I dry myself, my back turned awkwardly in the narrow wooden changing room, pulling jeans up over wet legs. I go and eat Greek food at a restaurant with Deb. I go back to Deb and Josh's house, sit on their sofa and watch *Modern Family* with Ruby and Leo. Younger than my two, they are sweet, thoughtful kids. Leo sits close as if he knows just how low I am, both of them laughing along, warm by my side.

And after Deb's, I pick up Josh and the kids, who are ambling home in the dark, flushed and happy with friends they have bumped into by the mosh pit. And I am so grateful for Josh, Deb, for their kids, for my kids. As I watch Mabel in our kitchen, hugging Jesse close, I hear her whisper . . .

'. . . Whatever happens at least we can still have fun.'

Hold on to this.

Hold on.

*

You are forty-six in two days. You are still in a coma. You have been asleep, oblivious, for three weeks now. But still, we decide to have a party in the square. This is the kind of mad antic, one of many that I will orchestrate, that underscores your restless hibernation. Where I, like some psychotic Red Coat at a failing Butlins, will desperately jig everyone along in the name of 'fun'. Jesse and Mabel, my constant allies, my comrades in arms, lug cold drinks and cake from the Waitrose in Brunswick Square to the now scorched grass opposite the National.

Bernard has made pinwheel sandwiches, and we lay blankets on the ground and the coterie of family and friends, constant and loyal, who visit you daily, drink champagne and cold beer and eat cake. Red velvet that, once cut, reveals rainbow layers of sponge. I am vaguely embarrassed, aware of how ridiculous it all is. A wedding without a bride. A funeral without the deceased. Part celebration, part vigil, you living somewhere in between, in this limbo, the pendulum swinging dangerously close, but not settling either way yet. My sister brings an illuminated letter J and rests it next to the cake. Jesse and Mabel are hanging with their cousins, and the teenage children of our friends, sitting on the square benches, swigging beer. Josh and Deb and Tash are away on holiday, grabbing the weeks while they can.

The roster of friends, good friends, Mattie, Nick, Mervyn, Ghiv and Kate, the few visitors who are allowed in, some individually, some in pairs, stand by your hospital bed and stroke your hand or say a few words. Your temperature is up again. The Rituximab, the immune suppressant that is meant to slow the NMDA antibodies, is not working.

Your numbers are still up. The rather dour anaesthetist, who has been in charge of your tracheotomy, catches me in the corridor. The EEG cap is back on, to measure the ever-fluctuating seizure levels that continue to permeate your watery sleep.

'The thing is, looking at him now, he looks like Jacob, but when he wakes up it is going to be very distressing, as he won't be the same,' he calmly warns.

This is the first time I have heard this. The first time anyone has said this directly to my face. I have seen, on the faces of the consultants and the nurses, a look that tells me all is not well, even though they profess calm. But this is the first time I have 'heard' it, understood it, beyond the late-night Wikipedia searches and medical papers I scour. No one else has been so honest. And I grapple with two competing emotions. One to smack him in the mouth. The other to cling on to him and never let him go.

Because I want truth.

I want honesty.

I want hard facts.

Not drama.

Not the fiction that I can assemble in my head.

But then he's gone, and I don't see him again, except briefly when you are awake again. Months later. And I see that look, the tears in his eyes, the relief and surprise. And I want to say,

'Look he made it. Look he's just the same.'

But we both know you're not.

*

Another dream, only you are not there to tell this time. I am alone, in our bedroom at the top of the house, with the hand-painted paper on the wall above our bed, which you argued over. I wanted stuffed birds, which you think are morbid. You wanted butterflies and bees. Butterflies and bees won. And pale pink walls. You said you wanted to make a bedroom for me. For me, who as a child had moved seven times before hitting my teens, there was a sweet logic to this. But still, I ask you why.

'Because I want you to know you'll be alright without me.'

These are the things that now resonate, the lines I turn over, rethink.

I am swimming in a pond.

I continue to go to Highgate ladies' pond a lot through this time, sometimes with Deb, sometimes with my dear friend Jane, who buys me a bright red swimming cap, that makes me look like something off a Busby Berkeley film, and I never wear. The ponds are a series of eight former reservoirs dug in the seventeenth and eighteenth centuries, that were dammed in 1777 to meet London's growing water demands. They're part of Hampstead Heath, my imagined resting ground. Legend has it that Queen Boadicea is buried somewhere nearby. According to legend, she and 10,000 Iceni warriors were defeated at Battle Bridge.

'At least I'll be in good company.'

Why didn't I think of that punchline when we were discussing the whole cremated/buried thing?

If only I had had that as a retort.

That would have seen you scattered next to me.

79

In truth, I find swimming there a little sinister. As the hot summer wanes, the evenings start to draw in. The dusky light through the trees is both beautiful and haunting. But it's what lies underneath that really scares me. Once, the larger pond, usually edged with anglers in their strange domed camouflage tents, was drained and old prams and getaway cars, tangled with duck weed, were revealed. Its dark depths unnerve . . . unsettle me.

I am swimming in a pond, in my dream. I know there are other people there but there is no one I can see. And I can hear you calling to me, from somewhere deep underneath. If I can just hold my breath long enough, I can dive and find you. I take a big gulp of air and dip down under the water. It is dark, cloudy, endless, and I am no longer in a pond. I am in the basin of the Hudson, named after the explorer Henry Hudson, cast adrift and never seen again after his crew mutinied. It's icy, and as I move, the water is slushy, almost tacky, and I realise it's starting to freeze around me. And I think—

'Of course, you're not here. You're on another planet. You've landed on another planet. Of course, you're not under here. Underwater.'

And then I'm awake, padding around in the downstairs bathroom cabinet, trying to find something that will help me sleep; amongst the Nurofen and paracetamol are the steroids I picked up that day, still in the box.

It is midnight. Past midnight. And I can hear voices. Mabel is in her bedroom talking to someone. Perhaps she's speaking to a friend, on Facetime. But it is late, and she should sleep. It's only when I get to her bedroom door that something makes me stop and listen, and I realise who she is talking to.

'. . . OK . . . anyway . . . that's just my day . . . OK . . . Daddy . . .'

It is months later that she will reveal she has been recording messages to you on her phone every night.

443 days of messages.

And we are only on day 50.

Friends continue to call, and I set up a WhatsApp group named 'Jacob's Buddies' to be broadened to include more people as the weeks roll into months: Bill, Baz, Damian, Holly, Annabel, Daisy, Anthony, Lucien, Stefan, Jamie, Nick S., Nick H., Mattie, Paul, Rich. The list goes on and on. A girlfriend says a Mass for Jacob, and Judith tells me the Rabbi at their North London synagogue has said *Mi Sheberach*, a blessing asking for compassion, restoration and strength. Jessica, wife of Robyn, a friend from Jacob's university days, has her entire Buddhist group chanting. She sends me a chant through the post. I try reciting it at night. The windows open, the August heat stifling. I leave the blinds up, terrified now of the total blackout darkness that Jacob loved to sleep in. Dorcas leaves her cellphone on, and when I am restless, fretful, unable to sleep, she lets me talk to her, waking her even if she is asleep. Even Daisy, the sister of Luke, Tash's partner, and a spiritual healer, is sending good vibes, offering to lay on hands. I take it all, open armed, gratefully. I am unashamed. I will do anything if it keeps you alive.

Neither Jacob nor I are particularly religious, though

culturally Judaism is at the core of who Jacob is. Holidays and high days are observed and enjoyed with relish. In the early days of our relationship, on Shabbat, the Jewish day of rest, either Bernard or Judith's house would host Friday night supper, a welcome respite after the exhaustion of parenthood at the end of the week. Chicken soup, matzo balls and chopped liver still a comforting, familiar balm. And when Jesse was born, we had a Bris – the religious ceremony where a baby is circumcised. In our sitting room, in the new house we have bought and can't afford, packed with our families and friends you have grown up with, who I neither recognise nor know, Jesse is placed on a cushion on Josh's lap. We have paid a mohel to carry out the incision. Jacob reassures me he is a doctor in the NHS.

Later I will wonder how I did not protest. Hormones, and a desire for Jesse to look like his father I expect. But when the children are older we will grapple more with our differing upbringings. I worry that our children will be confused with their '"Jew"ish' upbringing. I want absolutes. And answers. And to know who my God is.

Jacob reads avidly, Stephen Hawking and Richard Dawkins' *The God Delusion*, and argues with me when I challenge him on faith vs religion. Faith is about living with that which cannot be proved. Religion is everything else, from which you can choose to take the good bits. The sense of family, of community, of history, of order. The sabbaths and the celebrations. The challah, and the salt beef and the latkes and the fried fish. The customs and the rituals and the singing, that I find both confusing and enchanting, challenging and welcoming, a constant set of contradictions within which we live.

'I don't need to know who my God is. My God is science' always your retort.

'Black holes, and the Big Bang, is miracle enough for me.'

It's science that we have to trust in now. The consultants gather, looking over charts, tweaking medications, pondering over the mysterious graphs and printouts from the EEG, which raise questions as to whether the jagged rises and dips are seizures or brain activity. And always, always there's the sense they are trying everything. Puncturing and infusing and drawing blood and wheeling you for MRIs and CT scans. We're shown images of your brain during difficult consultant meetings. The hippocampus is 'bright' and 'vivid', confirmation that the encephalitis' work is not yet done. The front lobes are inflamed. There are days when they are not sure if you are fitting or waking. But it is clear when they say,

'Jacob's brain does not look like yours or mine anymore.'

We huddle as a family, staring blankly at these black and white images, constellations of shadowy cells and lunar lesions, that do not quite make sense, but which I know, if Jacob was sitting in the room with us, he would find magical.

'But is there brain damage?' I ask.

Nothing obvious yet. Nothing that they can see, they say, but not in a reassuring way, in a way that is non-committal.

We have to trust them. That the drugs will work. That they will solve this.

We have to live in the not knowing.

Make science our God.

There is a song by Tim Minchin, the comic and lyricist, which Jacob loves called *Storm*. He played it to me often, and it articulates so much of what he believes. Its wit and its grace in transcending the big questions of science and medicine floor me every time I listen to it. The author of the song has gone with his wife to friends, for a curry. A couple they know, who live in

Inner North London, top floor flat
All white walls, white carpets, white cat.

As the dinner progresses and tongues grow loose with wine, a fifth guest, 'Storm', newly arrived from Australia and a 'Sagittarian', covered with fairy tattoos, becomes more obstinate.

You can't know anything. Knowledge is merely
opinion . . .
The human body is a mystery! Science just falls into a
hole when it tries to explain the nature of the soul . . .
Pharmaceutical companies are the enemy.
They promote drug dependency at the cost of
the natural
remedies that are all our bodies need.
They are immoral and driven by greed.
Why take drugs when herbs can solve it?
Why use chemicals when homeopathic solvents can
resolve it?
I think it's time we all return to live with
natural medical
alternatives.

The author of the song can stay silent no more—

'By definition,' I begin,
'Alternative Medicine,' I continue,
'Has either not been proved to work, or been proved not
to work.
Do you know what they call alternative medicine that's
been proved to work?
Medicine.'

This song goes round and round in my head as I watch you lying in your bed. Lyrics seeming almost in time with the wheeze of the ventilator. Day after day, you're being pumped with poisons. While we wait for them to work, my mind is doing battle with a growing paradox that, increasingly, the consensus amongst the doctors is that it is a drug which was meant to help you, the monthly injections that you had for the last four years, and the withdrawal from that drug, that quite possibly, more than possibly, put you here. And yet we have to trust that it will be a drug that will save you.

Playing from the speaker above your bed that Jesse has magically got to work, the song concludes:

I am a tiny, insignificant, ignorant bit of carbon.
I have one life, and it is short and unimportant . . .
But thanks to recent scientific advances I get to live
twice as long as my great-great-great-great uncles and
aunts.
Twice as long to live this life of mine
Twice as long to love this wife of mine
Twice as many years of friends and wine
Of sharing curries and getting shitty at good-looking
hippies with fairies on their spines and butterflies on
their titties.

And this is how I hold onto hope, this is the mantra I chant
in my head—

> *Twice as long to live this life of mine*
> *Twice as long to love this wife of mine.*

Then one day I come in. I leave the kids in the waiting
room. We are allowed no more than two people in your
room at any one time. Your dad is just leaving. I cross over
to your bed and I say—

'Good morning, Jacob.'

You furrow your brow.

I move closer, and say—

'I love you.'

And you blink a little.

Your dad is amazed. You have done nothing. Given us
nothing so far.

The nurse tells me this morning, you tried to open an eye.

'I love you, Jacob. I know you can hear me,' I whisper
close to you.

And you move your lips a little.

The curl of your tongue seems to make the letter 'l'.

Trying to form the word, sending back a signal—

'Love . . . Love.'

4

It's October and I am in Florence with the kids. I turned fifty in September. You have been in a coma for nearly four months now. Jesse and Mabel had found a list on your computer of fifty things you were planning for me. One of them was a trip to Florence. Flights and hotel now booked, courtesy of my credit card, we set off for three days: Jesse, Mabel and me, because as Jesse says in his remarkable impromptu speech at another crazy act of 'fun',

'It's not enough just to survive, you've got to be able to live.'

Jesse delivered the line, which was apparently mine, at my birthday party, planned and discussed before your collapse, his glass raised to a long makeshift table of fifty friends and family assembled haphazardly in our kitchen, whilst you lie locked in the big sleep. I had wanted to mark this milestone some way, but perhaps even more than this, I needed Mabel and Jesse to see a roomful of the people who loved them, to know that whatever happened, there were others who cared.

'Did I really say that?' I ask Jesse after he has finished his speech.

'It's not enough to survive. You've got to live.'
Mentally I note it down, thinking,

'I am such a phoney . . . Doling out this shit . . .'

Words. Where do I get these words?

I am confident I have plagiarised the line from a film.

If not, I think, it's going in the final script.

Apparently I'd whispered the line to Jesse on the day he headed off to the Reading Festival, an essential rite of passage for any discerning North London teenager, after we had toasted shining GCSE results at Ciao Bella, an Italian in walking distance from the hospital, now our local. Before leaving, Jesse had hovered around your hospital bed, wanting to tell you the news, but not even the clutch of A*s makes you stir. It's a triumph to be pocketed, told later, enjoyed later. Another moment that you've missed. I take photos. Always digitally logging these milestones, an act of hope, that one day we will get to replay all the moments you've missed to you. That one day you will wake.

Occasionally you open your eyes, staring blankly. Or your lips move, or fingers ripple. Gavin, a friend of a friend, and brilliant barber who works close by, kindly comes with clippers and scissors and shears at your crazy hair and beard. We marvel at the sound of you chuckling to yourself, as Gavin trims, your eyes closed but smiling, still lost somewhere deep in your dreams. When Gavin blows the hairs off your eyelids and ears, you ruckle your nose as if caught in a cold breeze. They tell us you may still be able to hear voices, footsteps, the rustle of the living. So, we read, and sing, your mum and dad, sister, brother, Deb, me, Jesse and Mabel, your constant company. Jamie, an old school friend, comes in and plays his ukulele. Your fingers play along.

Time moves slowly in this unfolding story. The past is

another country, and now Jesse, Mabel and I are visiting it – literally. We both spent our gap years in Florence, just a few years apart, and we bonded over our experiences: me as a terrible nanny with an even more terrible family; you as a student, traveller and chef. It was the beginning of our mutual love affair with Italy, which we've passed on to our kids. This trip, mapped out by you, is now fully owned by Jesse and Mabel, who have thrown themselves whole-heartedly into the spirit of it, dragging me around food markets and galleries, like some ageing Denholm Elliott in our own *Room with a View*.

We jump queues and eat ice cream where we shouldn't and peer at the remains of Florence's most ancient Christian church in the Duomo's crypt with mild disinterest. We are distracted sightseers, caught between tourism and misery. And yet, there is joy and fun veined through our trip. We spend a mad afternoon making pasta and biscotti in the hotel kitchen with an earnest chef, we three, self-conscious as the real cooks work around us, prepping for the evening, trying to contain giggles as Mabel and Jesse are forced to smile and eat the 'chicken liver' crostini we have made and which they hate. A Michelin-star dinner, in a narrow bijou restaurant overlooking the river where salted silver anchovies arrive on a mini washing line fit for a doll's tea party, truffles are exquisitely balanced on puffs of pastry and monochrome caramels are served on a chequerboard, ready to be played.

Laughter and tears collide, as we walk giddily through the narrow Florentine back streets, Jesse and Mabel humouring me when I take them to the café I visited every morning over thirty years ago, before the misery of that terrible afternoon nannying job. I was eighteen, not much older than they are now. The café manager is kind and insists on the grand tour, showing us from table to kitchen. Perched opposite the bus station, I would cram myself with pastries covered in crunchy sugar and stuffed with custard, before taking the bus along the winding road up to Fiesole Piazza Mino. Later when Jesse was two, we rode around the city in a horse and cart. And we visited again, when Mabel was four and Jesse six, eating gelato on the Ponte Vecchio, where we lose them both for a heartbeat-skipping few minutes.

Back in August, in the early weeks of your coma, I take Jesse and Mabel to Puglia. Your dream house quietly bankrupts us with what seems like weekly bills for broken irrigation systems and tree pruning. It was always reliant on your renting it out and running it. Now it is a money pit, adding to a mounting financial strain that keeps me awake, restless and head scratching. Still, a few snatched days with Huw, my younger brother and his wife, my much-loved sister-in-law Sophie, and their boys, is a welcome relief, their boys Finley and Milo close in age to Jesse and Mabel. We cross paths with Dorcas, her husband Simon, and Harry, their teenage son, if only briefly. We swim and barbecue and I dip in and out, travelling back and forth to London to visit Jacob. Huw, chef extraordinaire, who has always seemed older in his love and care and support of me, sends me a photo of him with all the kids, standing huddled on a stormy beach at night. They have barbecued on the beach and this is just after. The rains there, cutting against the thick August heat, are spectacular. The clouds are dark and threatening overhead, and yet the night becomes an adventure for them all, a night that my kids still talk about. Captured in black and white, the cosmos ominous overhead, I pick it up on my phone. In London it is also raining. I sit by your hospital bed in soggy Birkenstocks watching you, your eyes open, staring straight ahead.

I think about the dark, thunder-clapping universe spinning in your head, which lolls as the nurses prop you up. Fingers rippling, you are repetitively blinking again. The NMDA antibodies at work, attacking your brain once more. They keep trying to take down your sedation, but you're struggling to manage your breathing, seizuring. So they put all three sedation medications back up. It is a setback. But we are used to setbacks.

We spin plates, as a family, communicating through a WhatsApp entitled 'Jacob Get Better', named in the early hours of Jacob's collapse. The essential carrier pigeon which we come to need and at times, I know, loathe. In short missives, or long diatribes, the daily gripes and glories are shared. Times of meetings, recordings of conversations with consultants, the observations, the reassurances when one or another of us can't visit, the sadness, the photos of Jacob, of missives put up by a ferris wheel of occupational therapists, physios and the speech and language team, as you start to stir. The criss-cross of family conversation, hurriedly typed en route to feeding another meter, or running to a meeting at work, circumnavigating, and at times exposing, the tensions and domestic politics that underscore it. I defy anyone to go through this experience and not, at one time or another, want to eat one's own head. To shout and scream. It is a mark of how strong we are as a family that we survive it.

Later, looking back at these texts, I see how brutal and savage I am at times. The feeling that you are owned by everyone, that I have to book an appointment to see you, makes me selfish, makes me angry, makes me forget that I am not the only one who is losing you.

'He's many things to many people,' your mother offers up one day.

I mull over this, unpick it, absorb what she has said. To me you are mine, you are the father of my children, my partner, my lover, my husband, my best friend. My tunnel vision all consuming, tenderly stepped around, borne by others caught in the full force of my wrath and pain. It shames me still, the times I forgot that you are someone's son, someone's brother, someone's friend. That love is not solely empirical. That there are ties of blood, bonds of DNA, of family that transcend twenty years of shared experience, walking side by side with another person. And yet you are woven into every fabric of my life.

I return to Puglia for a few days, and run into Giuseppe, our gardener, who wants to show me all the work he has been doing. Gruff, and hard to understand, particularly without Jacob's fluent, and with now only my bad, Italian. He gestures towards the vegetable patch and olive groves, with his usual brusque aplomb. But standing by a thin strip of curious scrubland, I look at him baffled.

'Jacob mi ha chiesto di coltivare dei meloni,' he replies.

Through a tangle of leaves, like something from a Richard Scarry book, tiger-striped, green watermelons and honeydews poke from twisting roots. Roughly translated,

Giuseppe has grown magnificent melons, a whim of yours now made real. I look at Giuseppe, and realise that the constant clearing of his throat that has punctuated the ream of words that have accompanied our tour, most of which is incomprehensible to me, is not, as I think, the dusty August air, but his attempt not to cry. Now as we stand, me marvelling at all the work it must have taken, all Giuseppe has achieved, we are both choked, over-wrought at this loss. The loss of the moment when he could unveil his beautiful garden to you. The loss of you experiencing this amazing thing. Later the kids and I cut the largest one we can find, and video it to show you.

'Grazie, Giuseppe.' We cheer as the watermelon cracks and almost explodes as it splits in two.

Judith is right. You are many things to many people.

Back in London, the Indian summer lasts well into late September. I punch the pillow at night, restless, and tell myself I have to get a new mattress, clinging onto the edge, trying not to roll into the deep indent on the left side where you would normally lie. I marvel every day how you can sleep, when sleep escapes me. Fentanyl, and propofol, pentobarbital, thiopental, is the pharmaceutical concoction keeping you asleep. Camomile tea and warm baths just don't cut it. Some nights the insomnia is so frustrating, I long for the sleep-filled coma that Jacob lies in, wondering if my heart, my lungs are strong enough to hold this.

I try and fail to move the bed which is still four inches from the wall and at an angle, from when the medics shifted it to try and move you. It weighs a ton and I wonder how we ever got it up here. The dog growls when I toss, restless, caught in the tangle of sheets and my feet. I think of the months you spent working not to let him onto the bed. The scratching at the door, the treats when he stayed in his basket on the landing. Then the victory when he stopped howling and at last slept downstairs. All blown within a few days of your departure.

I know how much you would hate the tiny changes, the subtle breaking of the rules. The purchase of another cushion. Another pointless chair. Another poster, with a hokey quote found on a new website. Layering our house with midnight purchases that I make on my laptop, face illuminated at 3 a.m. They've become a substitute for our nocturnal conversations when one of us would wake and nudge the other to roll over so we could share whatever pointless worry was niggling that night.

'Do you think we should get a different cover on that chair?'

'Do you think you should shut up talking?' you'd answer, spooning into me until one or other or both of us, too hot, will roll apart.

One Sunday morning Huw and I go to a screening of *Marriage Story*, an exquisitely observed, painful to watch, study of a relationship unravelling and the subsequent divorce. In the final act, the newly divorced Charlie sings *Being Alive* by Stephen Sondheim from the musical *Company*. It's off key, a little drunken and, given he's a theatre director and it's a last night party, suitably theatrical, but there is a brilliant moment when character and actor blur, and you feel as though you are there with Adam Driver in that bar, with anyone who has loved and

94

lost, but who doesn't regret it. Even though it leaves scars.

A few months before you collapsed I'd been asked onto *Desert Island Discs*. I have notoriously bad taste in music so I wrestled with being honest while being concerned with looking cool. I picked *Being Alive* as one of my final songs, dedicated to you. It was a toss-up between that and *Sorry-Grateful*, an earlier track from the same score. They both vividly capture the complicated nature of love, the state where you are 'always sorry, always grateful' that there is someone 'to sit in your chair and ruin your sleep'.

I miss you ruining my sleep.

Sometimes I wonder now if I willed what happened to happen. Because the dreams continue, and there is one that will linger and hover over me with an impending sense of dread.

You and I are hosting a dinner, although there are no visible signs of food or even guests. But people are coming, and Jacob is increasingly amorous, with family and friends, with shadowy bodies and unseen faces. He embraces them, showers them with compliments and praise. And yet – none of them sees me. Or worse – it is you who cannot see me.

I am invisible.

I am nothing.

I stand, watching as you work the room, the walls the same colour as my dress.

Did I know then?

Was some kind of future preordained?

*

Autumn, and slowly things fall apart around us. The lights won't go off in the kitchen. There is a sound of running water coming from the drain by the basement door, with no determinate source. The microwave has sparked and finally given up the ghost, defeated by a bag of instant popcorn which nearly burns down the house. The tumble dryer dies. White goods are shipped out and shipped in. There are cracks starting to appear, running from the living room to the top bedroom. My neighbour tells me he has the same problem and it's the fault of the sycamores on the rough patch of grass close to us, where once stood houses, bombed in the Blitz. We have to wait for the council to cut them down. One night I wake to a sound like a gun going off, and see the floor to ceiling mirror in the bathroom has cracked. The wall, moving behind it, has shattered the glass. There are bad omens everywhere.

The dog swallows a chicken bone, and it costs me £1,000 for an X-ray and medication.

There are days when I excuse myself to go to the bathroom, just so I can bawl. Sunday evenings when the chemistry homework and lost netball kits defeat me. When we need to buy Jesse his first suit. It is heart-breaking seeing Jesse watching TV alone. When my lame attempts at football commentary just won't cut it. The absence of you is overwhelming. There is a slow seeping realisation I have left so much to you. The banking, the car maintenance, the tax returns, the football fixtures and tutors, and vet appointments. The boring shit, that you picked up, sorted through, folded and put away, bringing order to the chaos, whilst I got on with my day. And so many bills and bank accounts are in your name. Note to self, do not let so much be packed away. Do not walk so blindly next to someone, do not so carelessly delegate that when they collapse you find yourself staring at a bunch of keys in a drawer, knowing that there are two storage units somewhere in London that they fit, but with no clue as to where they are.

I am defeated by our joint account, knowing neither the password nor username for that or for the account you set up that has the money I need to pay our tax. Suddenly out of the corner of my eye, I spot a curl of paper poking out of the bottom of a melamine notice board drilled to your office wall. I pull at it and discover several pages of pass-words, marvelling at how I have not noticed it before. It's almost as if you have nudged it a little, to make it easier, in some stupid game of hide and seek. The relief is over-whelming. Tax bill paid, phone bills, direct debits sorted, name of storage company identified. The top of your computer is baking hot, we haven't shut it down since you collapsed, months ago now. I scroll through the packed inbox of unanswered emails, largely junk mail, and reply like an incompetent secretary for both you and me.

The digital footprint you have left behind is both useful and painful. Photos and videos are reminders of all we have lost, always your voice and face just out of frame. I scroll through messages, emails, it's an access-all-areas pass. I come to love these notes, a window offered into the inner workings of your brain. Here are things you planned to do, school dates and lists of resolutions that you never kept. Characters' notes, long and fulsome as you grappled with a part, some I'd forgotten and which resurface like old friends.

Smith is awkward. Shy . . . I must try and embody that . . .

A single phrase—
It's Lily Cole . . .
Which you typed whilst we sat in the theatre together. You had smiled thinking you knew the tall auburn-haired woman sitting next to us, and I had enjoyed your mortified gaze when she looked back at you, benign yet blank. You typed it on your knee, flashing it on your phone to me, like a kid in a classroom who has just got the joke.

Underneath are the chords for *Somewhere Only We Know* by Keane, clearly to be learnt on the ukulele, to impress the kids, as they bash it out on the piano again.

And there's a list of symptoms, written days before your collapse.
Head Pain
Spots. Itchiness
Dizziness
Sickness
Eye pain
Blurred vision
Can't remember simple names
Struggling to concentrate. Learn lines
Cognitive problems
Nails purple
Shaking/trembles.
A list of things to be done to the house in Italy.
Pick olives
Call plumber
Pay water bill
Talk to Giuseppe – melons.
And then there is the list that you wrote in 2016.
Photos . . . lack of affection

Anger at my taking photos and videos
I was trying to capture my happiness . . .
A list to be returned to later.
To be looked at later.
The list of all the things Jacob disliked about me.
More than petty irritations.
Thought out, clasped tight in the knot of anger and resentment that lay side by side with the deep love and friendship that veined this 'marriage'.
The salt and the sweet.
The wax and the wane.
The gripes, that griped at us.
That we worked hard to tame.
Yes, to be returned to later. To be looked at later.
I have the dream again.

Mabel was two when Jacob and I first went to marriage counselling. Lina – six foot tall, German, with big hands. On our first meeting she looked at me and asked if I was taking vitamin supplements, warned that I looked pale. I guess the months of sleepless nights and breast feeding were finally kicking in. Jacob dug his nails into my knee, trying to stifle nervous giggles. Intimidated, we perched on oddly angled chairs, with nowhere to look other than at one another. Jacob had been a reluctant participant but when we retreated to the pub, we laughed and drank beer, vowing to give it one more go, out of politeness mainly. And we were running out of options, the months of takeout and a shared love of *Grand Designs* not quite cutting it anymore.

By the third session, we were devoted to Lina. On dark

autumnal evenings, with the kids in bed and a teenage babysitter clocking up the hours, we would drive, skidding along wet-leaf strewn roads that took us up and over Alexandra Palace and its glittering view, to this neat little white Georgian house, perched on the edge of the North Circular. Lina would be waiting, seated by a clock.

On a wall, she would pin a roll of brown paper, and each week we would write down the story of our lives for one another, Jacob on one side, and me on the other. Jacob nervously watching the minutes ticking by. What had triggered this visit? Arguments over education, music, the merits of laughter over misery? Wealth and poverty? Boundaries around family. Friends I liked, friends he loathed. If we could, we would fight over it. One day the anger was such that he punched a hole in a bedroom door.

Another afternoon, we couldn't decide on the positions of the sofas in our new living room. We kept tearing down the other's proposed configuration, until we sank down on the floor, heads flat against newly painted walls and wept.

What Lina saw and showed us was two young people, refusing to admit they were strangers, who had collided and bonded over sofa catalogues and baby rockers, and had completely skipped the part where they got to know one another. It was only as I was in labour with Jesse and we were arguing over potential names for him that I realised I had no idea what Jacob's second name was.

'What about Alfred . . . Alfie?'

'In Jewish culture you don't normally use a name of someone close who is still living?' he replies.

'Who do we know with the name Alfred?'

'Well, aside from my dad's cousin . . . Me?' he replied mournfully.

'Jacob Alfred . . .'

Forever Alfie to his friends.

We had never got drunk together, been on holiday together, shared a Christmas together, lived together, even had a proper, door-slamming, don't-speak-for-days fight together, before we got pregnant. We bought a house, merged bank accounts, merged lives, neither of us having ever lived with someone, other than friends or family. Together we cut our teeth on everything, including each other. We despaired often. We laughed often. We resolved things over a takeaway and a mutual desire to make it work, a determination to stick with it. And TV, movies, theatre, food, a shared love of Sondheim, and his ability to make me laugh at anything. Neither of us wanting to admit that we might just have made the most terrible mistake in mixing DNA without checking first if we two could even fit.

Over those weeks with Lina, we got to know one another. There was something quaint about the telling of our stories. The piecing together of our separate narratives, marking the fork in the road where our two paths would finally meet. Years later I will find our scribbled timelines, on brown paper, folded up to be packed away in a storage unit, to be found again one day in the future, when I discover where the hell the storage unit is. The convergence of our lives up until the point of meeting riddled with coincidences and moments of narrow misses. Lina talked poetically of trees and roots that grow together. We got pissed in the pub after and held hands and hugged one another gratefully. A near miss once more avoided. There was nothing we couldn't do now I knew he once wore purple dungarees. And in return, he delighted in discovering my career as a majorette in my early teens. Now we had pasts worthy of mutual emotional blackmail and public ribbing. The roadmaps of our lives, the people we loved, the break ups and make ups, the childhoods that had moulded us, shaped us, that tied us. We knew one another's secrets. The sheer act of visiting Lina meant we had at last a shared story, a shared history.

Outside it is getting colder and someone is leaving Jacob messages. A scattering of post-it notes stuck to the board, now filled with a collage of family photos. Messages of hope, written in beautiful curling handwriting, always marked with little drawings. A flower. A rabbit. No one knows who it is. Rumour is that it's a nurse from the rehab unit, but there have been no definitive sightings yet. But as the days go on, I see them everywhere. On different beds, in the corner of the waiting room, on a passing porter's trolley. A medical tooth fairy and we don't even have to hand over any teeth.

Jacob's sleep goes on, into late October. Though sometimes, often now, he seems to wake, body twitching, eyes opening, there but not there. They alternate the drugs, play around with his level of sedation, testing to see if he is ready to wake. But then the seizures kick in once more, you start the repeated blinking, the fingers flickering, and they put you back under. Still, they are hopeful you can hear us. You know we are here.

We circulate 'Jacob's Sensory Stimulation Programme' on WhatsApp. We are encouraged to keep talking to you, to keep trying to connect to you, even in your heavily drugged state. The conversation, the chat, the Sondheim played, the books read out loud to you, sometimes by an eager, short-haired lady; we never entirely know who has sent her but she seems to be some kind of hospital volunteer. Most days feel as though they are sliding into the void. All we do is try and stimulate Jacob and keep our sanity.

Now pinned on a board in Jacob's room is a list of—
Things To Be Aware Of
Overstimulation may result in flushing of the skin, perspiration, eyes closing, increase in muscle tone, tachycardic episodes. If any of these signs occur cease the activity immediately and allow rest period.
Ensure he is only receiving 10–15 minutes of stimulation followed by a period of de-stimulation, e.g. rest, turning off the lights, leaving the bay, silence.

I make a mental note to pin this up above my own bed.

One day on hearing Josh's voice, you open your eyes, smile, and your lips start moving as if you're trying to talk, which is something we are noticing more and more. You break into a sweat, cough, and gag, and often, when you become overstimulated, they have to suction you, which involves sticking a long plastic pipe cleaner down your tracheotomy hole. Every time I have to leave the room, it's ridiculous in the light of everything but I've had a fear of choking ever since childhood and it's the thing I hate the most. The kids mock me as I walk to the furthest corner of the ward and cover my ears.

The good news is, they are going to try a new drug, bortezomib, to see if this will control the storming that is targeting the NMDA receptors in your brain. Because as they admit, everything else has failed. It is a chemotherapy drug, an experimental approach that they have yet to get the funding for. But they have had good results in a few other similar cases, and are trying to source the drug, so we take this as a win.

We snatch consultations with the ever-changing carousel of consultants and doctors who come and go, who tell us this is a marathon, and it will take time and that nothing is certain yet. We nod and smile, and offer gratitude, but it is wearing, nonetheless. One day, one particularly young consultant asks how long Jacob had been in a wheelchair before this? I point at photos of him skiing on the wall, part of the collage of images that we have plastered on his notice board, a reminder to those who look after Jacob, and those who visit, who Jacob is.

And somewhere deep in me there is an internal snap.

'And he rode a motorcycle,' I say.

'And loves tennis.

And he plays the ukulele.

And he got an "Ology". He was the boy who got an Ology. In the BT ads.

You remember?'

They both look no more than twenty-five, these consultants. I doubt they were born when Jacob was in these.

But I go on—

'And he was performing at the National, this time last year.

Oslo? Did you see *Oslo*? He was the best Yossi Beilin. Ask anyone.

He was shooting a film, the week he collapsed.

And a TV thing the week before that.

He loves Old Fashioned cocktails.

And *The West Wing*.

And Tom Lehrer songs.

And over-expensive hoodies from Goodhood.

And lying in the hammock.

And football. Of course. His beloved Spurs.

And he can always find the best restaurants.

Pull you along on the best adventures.

And pastrami.

And mortadella.

And bresaola.

And salt beef.

In fact, he loves all meat. Bar liver. He hates liver of any kind.

And he speaks Italian, brilliantly. Fluently. Even though he says he can't.

And he likes opera. Not really opera. But the stuff he knows.

And musicals. He loves musicals.

And can sing Sondheim, badly and beautifully.

And a version of *I Won't Send Roses* that makes you cry. From *Mack and Mabel*.

And that's why we called our daughter Mabel.

Because we both love the music. Love the songs. Love the name.

And he loves De La Soul.

And N.W.A.

And he could be annoying.

And irritating.

And unconfident.

And stubborn.

But mostly.

He's kind. He listens.

And he has a laugh, that on the first time of hearing made me look at the people sitting behind us at the cinema, embarrassed, only to realise that it's the kind of laugh that triggers more laughter. That lights up a room.

A godsend in any audience.

A laugh that punctures everything.

And he can dance.

Did I say he can dance?

Not the stupid, moonwalk, funny walk dancing that I do.

That I always resort to.

That he would gently stop, when I would try it out on whatever dance floor we were on.

Really dance.

Pulling me close, spinning me around, putting me at ease, making me smile.

He is astonishing.

He's amazing.

He's beautiful.

And brilliant.

Brilliant father, brilliant partner, brilliant brother, brilliant son, brilliant friend.

He's not this.

He was never this.

He was fit and healthy and far from being in a wheel-chair.

Far from being any of this.

He is not *just* this.

He is *far* from *just* this.

But even if he had been, if he had been, if he was.

He would—

. . . still—

. . . be—

. . . all of the above.'

And they duly take note of it, writing it down.

They apologise.

They are kind.

They are young.

They are scared of me.

They scurry away.

And the monster crawls back into her hole again, sits back in her chair.

Watches Jacob sleep.

Some days, I want physically to climb on top of Jacob, slap his cheeks, and say—

'Alright, enough. This is just annoying.'

Because Jacob is pretending, and this is like one of those crap exercises I had to do as part of my drama course at university.

'Gather in a group. Now half of you lie on the floor and play dead. And the other half, you can't touch them but somehow you have to get them to wake.'

Sleeping Lions.

You are playing Sleeping Lions. And I am bored of it. So bored of it.

And then I put my fingers around your wrist, clock the shrinking.

You have lost kgs of weight and your legs look like sticks.

It's Yom Kippur. The Day of Atonement. The day when you would be fasting.

I lean in close—

'Mabel got new glasses today.'

And you missed it. You missed all of it.

And then I cross the room.

And when I do, you open your eyes—

. . . tracking me.

5

Hanukkah is early in December this year, and Bernard is in charge of latkes. I have memorised the Jewish festivals through the food. Pesach: matzah-ball soup, bitter herbs, a hidden matzo and a shank bone on a plate. Rosh Hashanah: apples dipped in honey and honey cake. Yom Kippur: you fast and no one can brush their teeth. Finally comes Hanukkah, which Jacob would declare 'the king of the festivals' – salt beef, latkes and donuts. And 'you get Christmas day as well' Jacob would chime to the kids. The upside to this whole Jew-ish thing. We barely notice the changing weather. I buy a Christmas tree that no one can be bothered to decorate, until I blackmail the kids and they drape some tinsel round its branches. There's a glittering fake tree in the waiting room, lights flicking on and off in an attempt at festivity. We have strung fairy lights around Jacob's notice board. The nurse's staffroom is bursting with cakes and pies, gifts from passing relatives. I hear Jenny, the ward sister, hungering for 'anything green'.

There is a new cycle of patients arriving, as others have left. Jenae, beautiful, just eighteen, on her way to becoming a make-up artist, now lies, like Jacob did for months, with an EEG machine strapped to her head. She had a stomach-ache, one weekend, which led to her dramatic collapse. Her parents and younger sister, always smiling, always stroking her face, hover by her bed. We exchange niceties, as the TV, punctuated with adverts for Christmas, plays overhead. Originally from South Africa, the photos on her wall confirm a life lived, not unlike our own kids, with parties, and selfies and laughing friends. The doctors are mystified.

Brian has been attacked by Guillain-Barré syndrome, an immune disorder of the nervous system, which has rendered him locked in, body unmoving, but for his eyes and lips that move in hushed conversation with Diane, his wife. She is soon to be a grandparent, has a keen interest in amateur dramatics, and we get to know one another standing in the corridor, side-stepping to our right and left, trying to keep out of the way of the nurses. Together we ignore the rest of the world, turning outside.

There are charity Christmas cards for sale on a table by MITU, facing the outpatient clinic. The nurses and doctors, with tinsel wrapped around their stethoscopes and trolleys, are fleetingly caught in view. Bernard heroically buys and distributes more chocolates and fizz for the nurses, meticulously remembering their names in cards. And in the chapel, at the end of the corridor, a hotchpotch of patients and volunteers sing carols. It is a curio of nineteenth-century stained glass with an ornate altar. Somehow this beautiful slice of the original building has been preserved, jammed amidst the scuffed Formica and scratched lino that makes up the rest of the hospital. It's a good place to sit. On bad days I light a candle, praying to anyone, everyone, but generally to the universe. When it is the call to prayer, nurses come in and pull out mats, angling them towards Mecca. Once or twice, I catch a porter eating his lunch.

Later, much later, you will sit and sing in here, Abba and Beatles songs, as part of your rehab therapy.

We have a hairy couple of days, your stomach is distended. They have stripped your clothes off again, wrapped you in an ice blanket. I call my sister and confide my fear you are going to die again.

It is Bernard's birthday and he's booked a restaurant close to the canal. Despite the tension and obvious concerns, we eat, and chat, and it is good to be together. The kids are happy to be with their cousins and grandparents. Everyone in both our families have busy careers, and they have been taking time out, day in day out, to cook meals, drive children, hug and hold us. They are the constant that keeps us going. That I will not get through this without. But it's been six months. All of us need to resume our lives.

And I have to write.

I am working on the second series of a TV show for the BBC. Divorce lawyers and their lives, it's an examination of love and marriage. I am literally held together by my brilliant executive producers, Jane and Lucy, and the show's editors, Emma and Clare, for the aptly named production company 'Sister'. Never will I feel that these women are sisters more: friends as well as colleagues, who constantly shapeshift their days to match mine, meeting in cafés close to the hospital or on standby to read scripts delivered at the eleventh hour. Letting me pass out on a sofa in a boardroom for an hour or more. Then ready, again, to stuff me with Haribos and tea and take notes as I cry, not sure if you are going to make it through today. And always ready to laugh at my conversation, laced with the black humour that is the companion to misery and the impending threat of death. Friends, good friends, part of the myriad of people who walk the dog, and deliver lasagne, and text, and ring, and just care. Meera, an actress and brilliant cook, drops in curries, that I spoon, cold, from the back of the fridge during midnight raids. And my neighbour, a lovely woman, who every Sunday, back from her weekend place in the country, leaves a pot of honey, a box of eggs, a bunch of dahlias on my doorstep.

I am aware this stuff could be boring.

That you, like us, must be tiring of this.

That this bit will never make the script.

The movie of this.

It will be a couple of scenes at best.

Possibly cut with a montage to include the walk on Primrose Hill with my mum and Mabel and ice skating in Somerset House in those last days of December.

And maybe with me circling the heath, mist low, dog in tow, looking mournfully at Highgate ponds, icy and freezing.

And of course, me picking up the jar of honey, tearfully smiling at the box of eggs.

But it happened.

It really happened. And what no one tells you about proper unfolding tragedy is that it is scary, and adrenalising.

But mainly it is boring.

The waiting is boring.

But I don't know how to get to the next bit until we're passed this.

Because in the film, we'll use euphemism. We'll blame the encephalitis.

But basically . . .

Jacob's stomach is distended, really distended, painfully dangerously swollen.

Basically—

. . . Jacob is full of shit.

The consultants look on anxiously, the danger that your bowel may perforate for a moment very real.

And all I can think is—

'This is no fucking way to go. He's not going like this.'

They decide to operate, and you are eventually transported to the UCH main building, only to be transported back again when they realise that surgery is too precarious. Your sedation is raised and they put you, once more, into a deeper sleep. All the while, the nurses quietly work, reassuring us that they have seen this before. Penny, lovely Penny, who I know has another, more interesting life, glimpsed when I see her without scrubs, whizzing past on her bike in brilliant vintage clothes, on her way to pick up her little boy, George. I buy her bike lights and some game with cats for George and bashfully leave them wrapped in a bag for her.

There is a strange kind of tenderness that you feel for the nurses, when the one you love's life is held in the balance, in their hands. When you know that they are the ones who have the power to shift the scales. The precarious scales, and just that 1 mg to the left can save their life. It is the NHS at its best. They massage Jacob's stomach, and roll his body, trying to get his legs moving while he's lying in bed. Then Penny has the brilliant idea of pouring mint tea through his feeding tube directly into his stomach, which seems to ease the inflammation and at last he shits.

It's as simple as that.

He stops writhing around in pain. His temperature comes down. He misses Christmas Day, but on Boxing Day he seems to smile as I talk to him, whispering and blowing kisses into his ear. The bortezomib is somehow working, delivered in cycles by Penny, who has to be specially trained to give him the injection in full PPE, carefully taking it from a metal box, like some sword of Excalibur, ready to infuse. And day by day we watch the pain ease. You ease. You are barely convulsing now, as they wean you off the sedation, little by little, every day until you start to wake, for longer, more fully. The consensus now is that it's more than likely that it is the drug you were administered to help your MS that triggered the anti-NMDA that has brought you here. And that the NMDA will stay positive in your blood for months to come.

I ask the consultants that come and go if they have tracked down the other patients, the other twenty-one spread across the globe, who have been affected by the drug. They reply that even if they could find them, it is all anecdotal, irrelevant, it's not a big enough test group to be able to make useful comparisons of care.

'But surely if someone has been bitten by the same snake, it's the same antidote that will cure.'

They tell me it doesn't work like that. And I nod, and act like I get it, but I don't.

And it stops mattering. Because you are coming back, you are pulling through.

We may have our Hollywood ending after all.

But still, it comes in bumps and starts.

You sleep.

You wake.

You silently stare, eyes travelling across the room, looking at the faces, the ebb and flow of nurses moving back and forth.

Then you sleep again.

In mid-January, you open your eyes, but this time keep them open. Then one day we come in and you are sitting up. The next you're smiling, responding more and wanting to talk, though you're still silent, the tracheotomy tube preventing speech. The third week in January, the day before Jesse's birthday, he is excited to tell you some news.

'Dad?'

I video it, you're lying in your hospital bed, eyes now wide, smiling at Jesse, who is leaning in close.

'I've got my provisional licence. I'll be able to drive soon, Dad.'

Your growl of contentment, audible through the tracheotomy tube, is like the purr of a cat. I look back at it often, replaying it, quietly marvelling.

He is back. He is here.

Even the doctors are happy. No more whispering in corridors. They greet us with an inner high five.

Or so I tell myself.

Or so I want to believe.

On good days, the nurses take you out, like some jolly school trip, wheeling you in a chair around the square, with a small entourage holding monitors and oxygen tanks. You bask in the sun, eyes closed, woolly hat and sunglasses on, still attached to a mobile ventilator. They tell us that you need less and less help and that you are getting closer to breathing on your own. A huge black padded Velcro strap, wrapped from the back of your wheelchair around your forehead to keep your head up as you sleep makes you look like some culturally inappropriate snake charmer or Middle Eastern despot. I almost wish you could see the comedy of it.

What no one knows is that, early in the month, when Jacob first starts to open and close his eyes, I go in to kiss him and he licks my entire face. It is unsettling, and beautiful and weird. He is using his tongue to feel his way, to explore the world again, like a baby. I am worried he may have gone blind. But the next day it is clear that his eyes are tracking people again. He is coming to. Coming back to life. His numbers, whilst still positive for NMDA, are getting better. It is the first time I believe that he will survive this. That he really will live.

'If I end up in a diaper. If I can't walk. I want you to shoot me.'

'I'd rather not,' I reply.

We are standing in our kitchen. Jacob is perched on a stool. Several months before his collapse. I think he's reading the paper. I am making breakfast. In a few minutes he is going to make me cry.

'I don't want you ever looking after me. If I can't wipe my own arse and can't walk, that's it. I am going to Dignitas.'

'How are you going to get there if you can't walk?' I'm getting irritated now. Plus, it is Saturday morning. How did we get here? It's not even ten.

'It's not illegal to take me there.'

'Do we really have to have this conversation now?'

'Yes.'

'Fine. But what about if I don't want you to? What if I want to look after you?'

'I don't want you looking after me . . .'

Later, months later, I will find Dignitas in the history on the search engine of his computer.

Next to Ocado and an article on nail fungus.

You are virtually off the ventilator and they are teaching you how to eat again. A balloon is inflated in your tracheotomy to stop you choking. Sue, the amazing occupational therapist, is an expert in feeding. I film you as she holds up a pot of hospital-issue strawberry yoghurt and you spoon it into your mouth, with surprising ease, sitting in a chair.

'How do you feel swallowing that down?' she asks.

You nod and smile.

'Good. Any itchiness? Any burning in your throat?'

You shake your head.

'And when you are ready, can I hear your voice, Jacob?'

'Yeah, you can hear my voice,' he quietly growls in reply.

Gruff and gravelly, a little like Luther Vandross, but unmistakably Jacob.

These are his first proper words for seven months.

Tears prick in the corner of my eyes.

I didn't know he would be able to speak today.

'Great, that is nice and clear. Lovely.'

Sue smiles, tall and elegant and rangy, like an encouraging games teacher.

I stop recording, flick the phone off.

'That's amazing, babe,' I say.

He looks at me sternly. Then turns away.

I have noticed this look in Jacob a few times over the last few days. Watching him grow in confidence, I tell myself it's because he is focused on relearning, on coming back into himself, his body. But even so, it becomes more pronounced as the days go on. The children are welcomed with a smile and I may get a nod.

In early February we take Jacob out into the square. He is now fully off the ventilator, largely silent, but occasionally he growls a few words. Escorted like the pope in his pope mobile, Ruby and Leo, Josh's children, are gripping the arms of his wheelchair. Mainly he smiles as he is wheeled around the wintery square, swaddled in blankets and scarves and hat. The family have come to witness, marvelling at the novelty of Jacob returned to the outside world. Bernard, Josh, Mabel and cousins tail Jacob while he, sitting crumpled under the blankets, filters our adoration through a blinking stare. Silent yet utterly there, he is squeezed and hugged and kissed by us all. But the star attraction is Styler, feverishly tugging at his fluorescent lead, sniffing the bins and snapping at fat pigeons. But on seeing Jacob, Styler springs to attention, and Jacob, as if at last remembering his cue, reaches out, trying to pull him close. Until we have to pick Styler up and sit him on Jacob's lap and he buries his face into Styler's fur. This is the grand reunion, both touching and a little odd, so profound is Jacob's love for our dog, clinging onto him tight as we resume perambulation around the square.

I film it all, and what embarrasses me most when I play it back to myself, is not just that I am talking to Jacob like a child, but that he is smiling at everyone, bar me. I notice that from time to time when I speak, he looks towards the camera, bewildered and a little irritated, until I am left standing with Penny, one of the nurses, and Brian, Jacob's fellow patient, also in a chair and along for the ride.

Back in his bed, later, a little tired and coming down from the trip, Mabel leans over his hospital bed, and sings to him. An Adele song, which he loves, her singing beautiful and rich, looking up at her adoringly as she strokes his arm.

'That was lovely,' he growls, his voice still rough from all the months of tubes and tracheotomy, with such focus on her it's as if he is trying to blot out the rest of the world. Once more, I film it on my iPhone, the quiet intruder, always watching him. He turns a little, as if he feels the invasion.

Is it my imagination that he glares at me?

Later, when I go to say goodbye, he won't reply, eyes fixed on the children, refusing to look at me. It is starting to become more than irritating; it is mildly disconcerting. Again, I tell myself, I'm paranoid. He's fine. He's just still waking up, like some grumpy, fat-bottomed bear.

A few days later, Jamie, his friend who plays the ukulele, comes to visit.

'Jamie's here, Jacob?' I say with a smile.

He greets Jamie warmly. Then raising a hand, but barely looking at me he says,

'Can you wait outside? Wait outside by the door please.'
Jamie and I look at one another, a little confused.

'Me? You want me to wait outside?' I reply.

'Yes, thank you.'
He's more insistent now.

'Yes please.'
Like he's talking to some over-attentive member of staff. I dutifully concede, standing outside, looking in, exiled between the medical bins and Brian, who is being suctioned in the next bed. I discreetly put my fingers in my ears. Jamie occasionally looks up at me, visible through the glass wall, like some mildly embarrassed parent whose child won't play nicely. I call my sister—
'He keeps ignoring me.'

Four days later, it is Valentine's. I go in with a bright red heart balloon and cake. For once, there is no one else in. A nurse I have not met before sits in the corner on a stool, quietly monitoring and checking his meds.
I enter and on seeing me she smiles, in anticipation—

'Look, Jacob. Your wife's here.'
He does not raise his head or look at me. She furrows her brow a little.

'Jacob. Look, she's brought you a lovely balloon.'
I tie it to his bed. I look at him and smile, hoping he'll find its cheesiness funny.

'Happy Valentine's, honey,' I say.
He looks up at the balloon, his face and the room perfectly reflected back at him, then back at me, with discomfort. I can see he's embarrassed for me.

Inside I am grateful I chose not to write a card.

The nurse nervously reaches for something by her monitor, trying to save the situation.

'Do you want to give your wife her present?'

She forces it into his hand, a red rose, wrapped in cellophane.

The cheap kind you'd buy from a garage or from a rose seller at a table on holiday.

A flicker board of Diptych candles and beautifully composed bouquets go through my mind. The care and the detail Jacob placed on celebrating Valentine's day varied. There were the meals at Scott's and the low-fly *Dirty Burger* days. Some years a swift peck on the stairs and a takeaway. Last year he gave me earrings presented in a restaurant halfway up a mountain, where we ate too much and groaned because we were sore from skiing. It didn't matter really.

'It's a made-up shit Hallmark holiday anyway,' we'd say.

But today, Jacob looks at the nurse, then back at me, gruffly takes the rose—

'Go on. Give your wife the rose, Jacob.'

. . . and lamely holds it out to me.

And then I see it. I know it to my core.

'She's not my wife,' he replies.

Technically he has a point.

'Husband . . . partner . . . husband . . . He's not . . . We're not actually . . .'

But even so. I shake for three days. I shake so much that

one day I ask someone if they can feel the underground underfoot.

Maybe that's it. Maybe that's what's making me tremble so.

I carry on as normal.

I mention it occasionally.

'Does Jacob ever ask you about me?'

And this is when it begins, the surprise, the look of bemusement, the disbelief from those who visit. I call my sister.

'Of course he's not forgotten you.'

The elephant in the room.

'This is crazy . . . So crazy,' she consoles me.

But I keep thinking of my dream, the memory coming back to haunt me again.

Another day he is sleepy, a little off, his temperature is raised.

Judith is in the room and he whispers something to me,

'This is my time . . .'

Later I discuss with her what he has said.

'His time to shine . . .' she has taken it as.

I hear it as a premonition of death.

Optimist vs pessimist.

Fantasist vs realist.

Of course he's not forgotten me.

'She's not my wife.'

Girlfriend. He meant to add.

'She's my girlfriend . . .'

And he will smile and say,

'She's not my wife . . . yet.'

But still the world shakes underfoot. Still, I grip the walls, in the morning, as I come down the stairs.

*

'What's your worst fear?' a friend asks me, a few months before Jacob wakes from his coma. At the time we are sitting in a corner of a coffee shop, run by ex-prisoners, close to the hospital. The coffee is good and there is a sofa in a window, where I watch the consultants and pale-faced visitors sit and drink lattes, the beans roasted in a prison somewhere in Hertfordshire. Redemption – yes that's the café's fitting name.

'That he'll wake up and won't remember me,' I say.

'I saw a film about that,' she replies with a smile and stands to get me another coffee.

Of course she saw a film about it.

It's a trope.

It's a cliché.

To be scored through by any eagle-eyed editor worth their salt, in red ballpoint pen.

'What would you prefer? That he doesn't know you or that he's dead?'

I ruminate on this at the time, mentally scoring this friend out with my own internal red ballpoint pen. I do this – to the truth speakers, to the audacious. I check them in and out, a little Marie Antoinette. Angry when they say the thing that I am thinking. Angry when they don't.

There are no winners here.

He can't have forgotten me, in other movies people forget people—

Total Recall.

50 First Dates.

Finding Nemo.

Memento.

Not this one. Not this one.
Eternal Sunshine of the Spotless Mind.
That's not how this one is going to end.

February: the kids and I are going skiing in Val Thorens. They have turned seventeen and fifteen in the last month. Debbie and Josh and Ruby and Leo come too. A week of throwing ourselves down mountains and hot chocolate. It's what I need. The mountains always clear my head. I was thirty-two when I started skiing, not including a brief trip to Slovakia when I was teenager, where I did very little skiing, spending most of the time snogging some spotty Italian boy on the roof of a rundown chalet. It was Jacob that got me on skis again. Buckling me in, pushing me on, skiing ahead, whilst I grumbled and moaned like some grumpy teen until, finally, he won, and I learnt. I ski now, nervously, with little aplomb. But I ski. And then when the kids were big enough, it was Jacob who got them, wriggling and protesting, into thermals and on the nursery slopes at the crack of dawn.

On the best holidays, we ski together, all four of us, through blue skies and white-outs and sleet. On the worst, I have torn or bruised something and greet them, flushed and beaming, in the hotel bar where I have retreated with laptop and a deadline. Jacob came to understand that it worked best when I had my laptop in tow, skiing in the morning, and letting them adventure in the afternoon. But this time, I crumble. Whilst Mabel and Jesse bomb down black runs and over jumps, I slide backwards down a slope, weeping and exhausted. I am out of puff. Out of sorts.

Held up by Josh and Deb who stoically steer us through the holiday as WhatsApp messages keep us updated on Jacob's progress.

In the early days of Jacob's waking, the physiotherapists stand him in a frame that keeps him on his feet and upright, head held on a chin rest. He pats a balloon from left hand to right, slowly and carefully, but not without precision. Some things are coming back with relative ease. One day he speaks to Judith in Italian. Another he wolfs down asparagus and salads Bernard and she have brought in from home. Tash downloads films on his iPad. He is watching *The Kominsky Method*, though his short-term memory comes and goes, and he is never entirely sure what episode he is on, so he watches them more than once. He is taken to the square again, this time with his dad and Tash, and is once more reunited with Styler. Jacob's attachment to Styler, our crazy Labradoodle, seems unconditional, he's always holding him tight as if not wanting to let him go. When we're back from holiday and take Styler to see him, there's the same ardent connection, and I bristle a little, with jealousy.

I am jealous of the dog.

I have hit a new low.

They take out Jacob's tracheotomy, the hole covered by a plaster, which quietly fascinates me. There is one day when he seems to be breathing through it, the plaster rising and falling a little when he speaks, only occasionally, but he answers when prompted. We start to write the names of the daily visitors down in a diary, so that he can keep track, keep hold of the days, what he's done. An old-fashioned A4 black book, that gets increasingly bashed over the weeks and months, nestling next to the endless grapes and biscuits and newspapers that we bring in for him to read.

And at last, the magical word – rehab – is raised.

'Jacob is moving' I WhatsApp everyone excitedly. Initially he'll be in a room on a ward close by, whilst we wait for a bed. Sue, Jacob's life-giving, yoghurt-feeding, miraculous speech therapist, smiles encouragingly. This is a good thing. A good sign. He is leaving MITU.

'Isn't that good, Jacob?'

Jacob nods and smiles.

'Aren't you pleased?'

Jacob nods then frowns at me.

'He's not sure,' I say

'Of you. I'm not sure of you,' he replies.

And so, it begins.

The not knowing.

He would have to know me to forget.

And slowly, surely it becomes apparent, it's not that he's forgotten me. He doesn't know me, can't locate me, something I piece together a little more each day.

I print out a clutch of A4 photos of us all, individual faces of everyone in the family, and ask someone to pin them around the bed. When I come in the next day, all of the photos are up on the wall around him. Except mine, which he doesn't want up. He conceded, when pushed, to have it stuck behind the sink, out of view, far to his left. Sue asks us to make him a book with a simple set of statements and photos. To help him remember, locate us and himself.

'Who am I?' reads the first statement, a photo of Jacob on the facing page.

'This is Jesse, my son. This is Mabel, my daughter. This is Abi, my girlfriend . . .'

I notice he flicks over the page of my photo, quickly, every time.

I ask him why he does this, and he simply says,

'I don't know her.'

Then he looks at me, silent, almost goading.

'She's Abi,' I reply.

'No, she's not,' he insists.

I feel sick and curious. It's a weird conflict of emotions that accompanies the shock and pain of Jacob's odd revelations. But maybe it's not so surprising. There's a fascination in understanding that which is deeply upsetting, a desire to get it out, to look at it, to see what is upsetting.

'So, I'm not Abi.' I push a little.

He shakes his head.

One day I record our conversation, my iPhone camera pointing at my feet. I have stopped caring about what I am wearing. My socks are odd, poking out of my scuffed white Converse trainers. It follows a now familiar course. I say something about being me and he will dispute it. I then defend who I am.

Or challenge him,

'Where do you think Abi has gone?' I ask.

My legs crossed, my foot nervously tapping, the scuffed lino underneath, the only thing in shot.

'She's gone away with someone,' he offers.

Listening to the recording again, I have forgotten that the growly voice he had when he first spoke has evolved a little.

Now he sounds like a really boring carpet salesman from Norwood.

'Really? Why would she go away with someone?' I say. I can't believe I have started to refer to myself in the third person.

'Because she's started a new life,' he decides.

God – this is ridiculous.

'Right . . . OK . . . Well, remember what we said about your brain having an infection.'

'Yeah . . .'

'And all the files being dropped all over the floor of your life. And you're picking them up, each one, and one of the files . . . That's me. And when you learn to pick up that file, I hope you'll see that I am Abi.'

'No, you're not,' he mutters.

'OK, that's fine. But I am Abi,' I say.

The neuropsychiatrists and psychologists now working with you have told me not to try and dispute your rationale.

'You're not,' he replies.

'Yes I am.'

The ping pong of words that I push until one or other of us tires of them.

'Not.'

'Am.'

'Not.'

'Am.'

Later, Dr T, Jacob's slightly nervous psychiatrist, always on the back foot, always looking terrified that I am going to stop him as he whizzes past, will encourage us to work on Theory A and Theory B. Sitting in the side room that is part staffroom, part corridor, and hot and sticky as the rest of the hospital always is, Dr T posits,

'Theory A – Jacob you are right. She is not Abi.'

This is early on in one of the sessions that I have been invited to. Later, I'm no longer invited, because Jacob would prefer I am not there. Or Abi Morgan as Jacob will come to refer to me. Me being the real Abi who is not me. He will only ever refer to that Abi as Abi Morgan. He hasn't yet decided what to call me, the imposter.

'But we always have Theory B, Jacob,' Dr T continues. 'We can never be entirely sure of anything, so let's say you, Jacob, are 99 per cent right. You can never be 100 per cent. So, let's start to think in the realms of possibility that there is 1 per cent chance that this is Abi Morgan.'

Jacob stares blankly back.

'Can you go with that?' Dr T says, nudging the words hesitantly forward.

'No,' he replies.

Twice as long to live this life of mine . . . Twice as long to love this wife of mine.

'Are you sure, Jacob?'

'Yes.'

He never can.

I have been rubbed out.

6

It's March. I am going out to dinner in a private room in a nice restaurant in Soho with the actors in *The Split*, the show about the divorce lawyers I've been working on. It's a welcome hurrah before the start of filming. I stop off to see Jacob in his room, now on a ward, still waiting to go into rehab. He has been in hospital for 275 days.

'I'm going to see the cast from *The Split* tonight, Jacob.'
'No, you're not,' he replies, eating grapes, lost in watching Benedict Cumberbatch give his all in *Sherlock Holmes* on his iPad.
I record him on my iPhone again.
'I write *The Split*,' I offer up.
'No, you don't. Abi Morgan does.'
Earlier he tells me that they will have to adapt 'his' flat.
I ask him where his flat is.
'Hampstead.'
At least he has imagined somewhere nice.
This delusion won't last long, but it does amuse me. We have discussed moving to Hampstead when the kids are older. To an apartment overlooking the heath. In his mind, he has already done this. Without me.

A few weeks before this, in the days before Jacob left MITU, I come in with a smoothie, which he takes and calmly drinks. Then, very quietly, he says,

'I don't know how you are doing it, how you're convincing everyone you are Jesse and Mabel's mother, but I know you are not who you say you are.'

'Who am I, Jacob?'

He looks at me, eyes pooling with tears, staring off into the middle distance.

'Why do you have such an interest in my children?'

'They are nice children,' I reply.

'Do you like them for something else?'

I look at him confused.

'What do you mean?'

Then it dawns on me— 'Sexually?' I proffer, disturbed.

He nods.

Before I can respond, the smiling, short-haired volunteer lady, who reads aloud to random patients, hovers irritatingly by the door.

'Hello, Jacob. Shall I read your book to you now?'

'Yes please.'

It all feels like a bad episode of *Westworld*, the dystopian Western meets science fiction TV show we were both quietly addicted to. The resemblance with one of the creepy android 'hosts' is unsettling.

I take my cue from his silence. He's now absorbed by the reading lady, perched on a chair, as she ploughs into *The Princess Bride*, turning the pages on the copy I bought after his old paperback fell apart. The copy I gave him two Christmases ago and brought in because I know it's his favourite book. I leave, the world once more shaking underneath my feet.

There is a short piece of footage of Jacob, taken that same Christmas, 2016. It lasts for thirty-four seconds. It is of Jacob opening a ukulele case and removing a walnut ukulele I have just given him. He is standing in our living room, smiling with obvious pleasure. Fred Perry T-shirt, rolled-up jeans and scuffed Stan Smiths.

'Oh my God. It's so sexy . . .'
Jesse and Mabel are singing in the background as he strums a few chords . . .

'And out of tune . . .' he laughs.

Thirty-four seconds of Jacob's pure pleasure. I play it over and over again. On the worst nights. On the loneliest nights, when I wonder if I am going mad, blindly navigating my own dystopian nightmare, this video, this video is a touchstone that tells me I am sane. It was real. What I was to him did exist. I got it right. Years of inappropriate presents but one year, the ukulele . . . He loved it. Loved me.

I am not mad.

I will not go mad.

In Jacob's Therapy Discharge Report, when he finally leaves the hospital, it will say of this time—

By mid to late February, Mr Krichefski was noted to experience visual hallucinations and fixed delusions regarding his partner. While he has insight into the disturbing hallucinations, he does not waver on his belief that his partner is an imposter (Capgras syndrome).

The notes confirm that initially the children had slipped his mind too. It was something I had been concerned about, but had quickly dismissed, even though he had asked me,

'Who's that girl?'

I sternly told him that she was Mabel, his daughter, and not to forget it. He had dutifully nodded.

But then he remembered them.

To forget them, that would have been too much to bear.

Capgras syndrome. Way before we have the report, it's Jesse who first suggests it as a diagnosis – my addiction to late-night internet surfing, to discovering information that will crack this nut, now transferred to him. I Google it and find a series of very bad student films, largely in Spanish, that go a little like this.

'Hola Manuel.'

Two students meet in a café, it is very badly shot.

'Hola Juan.'

'Qué tal tu día?'

The two students awkwardly sit, drink coffee and 'casually' chat. Cut to a second scene, same students, same scenario, the scene on repeat.

'Hola Manuel.'

Only this time the other student looks at his friend blankly.

'Perdón te concozco?'

Then walks away. Manuel looks on, disturbed, scratching his chin.

Bad credits follow with creepy music.

Note to self, if you are a psychology student don't act in your own films.

This is about as good as it gets for Capgras syndrome, named after Joseph Capgras, a French psychiatrist who, in 1923, was the first to identify this delusional misidentification syndrome. I will later learn that Jacob is only the second case in the world where the syndrome originated with encephalitis. The other is a man in Japan, who does not recognise his wife. He never recovers. It normally affects those with dementia, those older than Jacob, and mainly it is found in women. Also known as 'imposter syndrome', this psychiatric disorder can display itself in other forms. Normally the object of the delusion is the spouse. But the person experiencing the delusion may believe an animal, object or even a house is an imposter.

In the case of 'Madame Macabre', Joseph Capgras' patient, she believed her husband and other people had been replaced with a series of 'doubles', a behaviour he initially dubbed 'Illusion des sosies', which literally translates as 'the illusion of lookalikes'. Though curiously, when I ask Jacob what Abi Morgan looks like, Jacob insists that she is tall, with long black hair and blue eyes. My eyes are brown, my hair shoulder length, also brown, and at a push I can scrape up to about five foot two. Another strange aspect to his delusion. Sometimes it is as if he plucks things from the air.

I find a short film on YouTube, part of a bigger documentary. A young man, I think also Spanish, no longer recognises his parents following a car crash. Unable to care for himself, you see him happily sitting down with his mother and father, looking at old photo albums, moving between a flat in their basement and their apartment above. The mother explains to the camera that while they have found a way of living with it, the closeness, the warmth that she once had with her son, is gone. He no longer identifies her as the mother in his memories.

I try bargaining with Jacob. One day I suggest he quizzes me – favourite foods, favourite football team, favourite holiday. I get every answer right. Rather than being amazed, he stares quizzically like a member of an audience in a magic show, trying to work out how the conjurer has managed to swipe his watch and is now wearing it on his wrist. A look of impressed distrust, that I will get used to.

Another time we talk about our children's births. I remind him that he fell asleep on my hospital bed after Mabel was born, next to his tiny new daughter. I sat eating Marmite on toast and drinking tea at five in the morning, watching them both. Truly one of the happiest moments of my life. Talking about the day, I let him run free, enjoying the memory, pitching in occasionally until I admit—

'It was an amazing day.'

'Yes, it was . . .' he replies, smiling at me. 'I wish you'd been there.'

Sitting with the actors of *The Split*, having finally got to my dinner in an upstairs private dining room of a cool Soho restaurant, I spill, unable to contain the news. I have verbal diarrhoea trying to comprehend what is happening. I seem deranged, spooning food onto my plate, blindly eating, starving, but barely drawing breath. Stephen Mangan and Nicola Walker, brilliant as well as talented people, are kind and humour me. I must seem nuts. This is the way it will go. I will steer conversation with anyone I can find, anyone who will listen, to reveal what is happening. Like some mad chattering stand-up, honing my act, working out where my story flags, getting kicks from the laughs, the hits. Friends, colleagues, family, neighbours, our cleaner. I realise I have to stop when I share everything with the barista at my local coffee shop, a bewildered Italian boy who smiles and nods politely and gives me a croissant for free.

My day job is to create characters. Whether they're based

on real people – and over the years I have written screenplays and stage plays, peopled by Margaret Thatcher, Charles Dickens, Emmeline Pankhurst, Nelly Tiernan – or fictional. I have plundered the depths of research to create murderers, psychopaths, sex-trafficked women, pimps, sex addicts, war photographers, nuns, detectives, news reporters, journalists, suffragettes, soldiers. The summer that Jacob collapsed I was working on a drama about the life of Cleopatra for Netflix.

Actors often ask for character breakdowns, and I write them in retrospect, long after I have written the script, often checking back on scenes, in search of detail. Character traits that I haven't even considered are often revealed on re-reading. I am surprised sometimes at how bold I am in my unconscious choices and how actors commit to them. They are my creation, I can give them a hump or a limp, a childhood neurosis or a fetish. And actors will take these pages and miraculously channel them as only actors can, utterly inhabiting and adopting these asides as their own, until I no longer know if I am the birth or the surrogate mother. But this, this is different. The role I have written, that I have created, that I have performed my entire life, is now being challenged. I am a bad actor, the wrong actor, in someone else's part.

But I'm not ungrateful. Not entirely ungrateful. There is a mawkish fascination in watching how life is starting to unfold. How Jacob sees the world and me.

I am not blind to the old adage . . .

'It's all material . . .'

This will be said to me, several times by several people. And it's not that I am not, in my head, already moulding,

136

shaping, constructing this plot, this narrative, this unfolding script. I am mercenary, parasitically enjoying every new moment, recognising that there is a good story here. I experience every new punch and blow with a kind of masochistic fascination. I mentally asterisk and file it under <u>To be looked at later. To be researched later</u> with all the other *New York Times* and *Vanity Fair* articles I have collected over the years. Torn pages ripped from waiting-room magazines and airplane freebies.

'Everything is material, right . . .'

But this, this is a little too close for comfort.

The worst is when I am meant to smile, enjoy the wry aside when visitors, normally those I don't know that well, distant friends of relatives, nervous and not sure what to say, come up with the brilliant notion that somehow there is a silver lining to every cloud—

'Well, you can fall in love all over again.'

To which I rudely, cruelly, sharply reply—

'An unemployed actor currently incontinent and in a wheelchair would not be my date of choice.'

I am not great company.

I snarl.

I growl.

I am sorry for myself.

I angrily WhatsApp.

I cry a lot of tears.

Jesse stays calmly rational. Mabel grips my hand, strokes my arm, feels for me, painfully.

Reading back over the texts, I can see how hard Jacob's family worked to be kind, to be sensitive to me.

But I am raging. I am a ball of rage again.

I look up the definition
Rage – violent uncontrollable anger and/or a vehement desire or passion.
I have one particularly mad day when I become convinced that all the affection Jacob spills on Styler is misplaced, and meant for me.
It is weirdly comforting.

In late March Jacob is at last moved to rehab. Jacob lets me accompany him, coming to accept that I am some kind of person who has been appointed, quite possibly by the 'state', he offers up one day, to look after the children and him. A few days before, in a café housed in an old church across the square, I meet up with Dr O, a friend of Deb's and one of the head consultants there. We sit eating cake and drinking coffee, smiling nervously at the Rentokil man laying traps for the mice. Dr O is kind and calm, and quietly reassuring. He has seen remarkable examples of recovery.

Hope is reignited once again.

Rehab is part care home, part *One Flew Over the Cuckoo's Nest*, not the Four Seasons we hoped for. There's a single floor in the main part of the hospital, bridged by an ornate stone staircase, that houses a gym, a little like one you'd find in primary school, a dining room and a TV, where blank staring patients paint and work with therapists on puzzles. We all quietly mourn the peace and calm of MITU, as Penny, Richie and Keisha unpack Jacob's ever-increasing belongings into the standard hospital-issue side table.

It's dinner time, and as Jacob eats the Leon meatballs I have brought in, others pick at shepherd's pie, in microwave trays, in the communal dining room. I smile at the man sitting opposite me. Almost comically tall, he's in his sixties, with a shock of grey hair that makes him look as though he has stuck his fingers in an electric socket. He has a touch of the Lucian Freud about him, legs crossed, head cocked at an angle, and I imagine, in another life, a small roll-up squeezed between two fingers. He stares back at me, a little suspiciously, one eye so heavy lidded it seems almost sealed, but with the other he looks at Jacob with a knowing smile and says, in broad cockney—

'I bet you want to get her home and fuck her.'

Nice.

Jacob looks back, unamused.

Everything is wipe-clean here and just a little bit sticky. Jacob is wedged into a corner bay, barricaded by a glass panel, looking out over the narrow corridor, bang next to the nurses. Next to him, Robert, a rather elegant-looking man, clearly recovering from some debilitating condition, will smile and nod occasionally at Jacob. Jacob pointedly ignores him. Later we will discover Robert is a psychoanalyst. I wonder what he makes of this place. This is a club that if it wants Jacob as a member, he doesn't want to be in. Weirdly, it may just be the saving grace for all of us.

Because Jacob needs me.

For cake.

For conversation.

To download films.

To bring clean T-shirts and take old ones away.

For cold smoothies.

For Itsu coconut chicken soup.

For the newspaper. *Guardian* in the week. *Observer* at the weekend.

To read him texts from his cellphone.

To organise the wheely tray table, that swings over his bed and has an ever-changing Eiffel tower of books, grapes, Top Trumps, nail clippers, reading glasses and chocolate that friends and family bring.

To puncture the monotony.

To congratulate him as he moves from bed to the gym. A narrow corridor of mats and bars and weights, where Jacob learns to stretch and lift, and build his muscles again.

Every day, he is washed by a nurse and dressed in joggers and trainers, and escorted, first in his chair, then with his walker, finally shuffling himself.

He refuses to talk to anyone. But we all keep coming – Bernard, Judith, Josh, Tash, Luke, Deb, friends, my family, Huw, Dorcas, my mother, Patricia – rushing across town from work, or meetings, juggling lives to come in with meals and books and conversation.

In turn, Jacob is worked every day. He has occupational therapists who teach him how to clean his teeth, make a cup of tea and wash a mug, reconnecting him to old domestic migration routes. With the physios, he makes progress from pulling himself up, to walking up and down stairs. His legs grow stronger, and I am amazed how quickly the muscles build around once spindly thigh and shin bones. Speech therapists try and work on his breathing, to bring more inflection to the monotone he has developed. Dr B, a smiling, slightly aloof, yet down-to-earth neuropsychologist, tries to navigate Jacob's fluctuating mental state. Sometimes he talks out loud, or moves his arms, miming drinking or driving in his sleep. The medications are rebalanced, epilepsy medication fed back in when it has been taken out too quickly. Yet still there is a mystery to Jacob, he is back. Yet not back.

One day, Dr T passes me, as ever in a rush. And then stops. A genius thought has just come to him.

'Did Jacob ever want to leave you?'

I hesitate.

'Not that I know of. I mean . . . we had our moments but . . . Not that I was aware of.'

'Hmm . . . It's just in 80 per cent of cases it's found the person with the delusion actually wanted to leave the relationship,' he replies.

And then he's gone.

'80 per cent . . . ?' I think.

Five years before Jacob's collapse, I was nominated for a glamorous gong – an Emmy for a show I had written for the BBC, *The Hour*, made with my brilliant producer and friend Jane Featherstone, again. I wasn't going to win. But Jacob and I decided to make the trip anyway. We stayed four nights at the Sunset Marquee in LA. They upgraded us to a bungalow. The bellboy, a cool out-of-work actor in his forties, befriended us. We got perks. We grazed the endless buffet in the water-edged breakfast room. We wined and dined, and tripped around Hollywood, giggling and having ridiculous fun. On the day of the ceremony, I squeezed into a dress, and terrible shoes, and we sat in our limo for hours, on the slow crawl to the awards. What no one tells you about these events is that if you are not the star and a size o, no one is clamouring to dress you. And I am a chaotic shopper, leaving most things to the eleventh hour. I pray no one on the red carpet asks me what designer has made my dress, cursing that I haven't taken time out to think ahead. Jacob looks considerably more dapper in his black tuxedo. I make a mental note not to do this again. But luckily, as is often the way, the writer glides past happily unnoticed, cameras flashing and microphones waving at the stars, Hollywood's gods and goddesses.

We have both been to this kind of event before. But even so, the people-watching is always fun. For me it is the writers that blow me away. Stephen Levitan, writer, director and producer of *Modern Family*, is sitting behind me. Vince Gilligan – *Breaking Bad* – to our right. Aaron Sorkin to our left. As ever, there are few women. There will be. But not yet. There is also never enough to drink, and endless categories and not even the juice box they have put under our seats can quench our thirst. Plus, we are starving. So starving. I munch on an old biscuit I have hidden in my bag, nicked from the hotel.

At last, 'best writer for a limited series' comes up, and I am already trying to work out how long it will take to get an In and Out burger after this. Then they announce the winner. And it's me.
It's me.

Jacob is nudging me ecstatically, and I'm looking at him, confused and panicky, as he pushes me up to standing. I stumble towards the stairs, in my glittery dress and ugly shoes. They are from Clarks. I don't know why I wore them. I was under the illusion they would be comfortable. They're not. The whole shebang is utterly surreal, and, as I grab the award, presented I think by Allison Janney and Anna Faris, even Ms Faris, who is no skyscraper herself, has to bend down to hand it to me. I turn, a sea of faces, the great and the good staring back at me, my mind blank—

'Fuck . . . why the fuck didn't I write a speech?' I think.

And I swear I can see Michael Douglas, amazing this particular year in his turn as Liberace in *Behind the Candelabra*, which revived his career and is clearly Emmy worthy, I can see he is clearly trying to work out how I have won it and not the writer for his thing—

'Who the fuck is she?' I swear he mouths to the guy on his right.

Headless, I stumble through a few obvious thanks, working my way through a rambling, plucked-from-the-air list. And then I have the genius idea, midway through talking, to pull out a 'witty' anecdote that happened to us flying in. It's a gamble. But this is it. This is my moment. At LAX airport, the immigration officer had questioned if I was really going to the Emmys.

There is a fleeting thought, midway through the story, when I realise that I have one of two options: hit the punchline or thank the most obvious person, who I have missed.

'I guess they're going to have to believe me now.'

Boom . . . Boom.

I smile, arm raised, waving my Emmy gratefully.

And that's it. And within seconds I am shuffled off back-stage to a series of impromptu press interviews, before I am

143

ushered back to my seat, in a haze of people patting me on the back and congratulating me, including Jacob.

And I didn't do it.

I failed to do it.

I failed to thank the person I love the most.

Jacob.

I bumped him for the hit of the funny.

Afterwards, I apologised of course, and he is gracious, quickly dismissing it. We party and discover that if you walk around with an Emmy everyone loves you and smiles as if you are a new-born. But if you leave your Emmy in the limo, which we did by the fourth party, you are a nobody. Nobody looks at you. Or smiles at you. It was noted and quietly levelling.

We danced all night, until the swirling carpet at the HBO party defeated me and Jacob had to steer me home. But not before I had grabbed several members of *Breaking Bad* and *Girls* to fangirl. Jacob literally had to unpeel my fingers from the nerdy guy who goes out with Lena Dunham's flatmate and works in the coffee shop. It was a great night, trippy and memorable, and it took us three days to recover from the hangover. I woke up with chocolate on my face, still in my Spanx, hyperventilating, they are so tight around my stomach and hips.

The following day, Jacob hired a Harley and we drove down to Malibu, ate crunchy crab cakes and lobster overlooking the foaming Pacific. We stopped to visit glamorous friends and had martinis and dinner. We headed back to London, Emmy in hand, a little dented from where I had dropped it on the way home from the HBO party. And though Jacob smiled and insisted it was fine, we both knew that there was a crack, a fault-line, running through our relationship, that had always been there, threatening. And that it had just opened up that little bit more.

A few months after, we went into therapy together. Again. Years on from Lina who we still talked about and smiled and remembered. This time was different. It took two years for Jacob to really forgive me. It didn't look like much. An understandable slip.

But it said a lot.

Revealed a lot.

The quiet tell.

I had let go of the hand of my running partner.

I had run on ahead.

I had crossed a finishing line without looking back.

Jacob, my constant support. The one always cheering.

And it would come back to haunt me.

Still haunts me.

That's when he wrote that list.

The list I found on his phone.

The list of things he was angry about.

'I want you both to make a list of what you are angry about.'

Lynne . . . The marital therapist's name is Lynne.

I never got around to writing mine.

He obviously did.

It is too painful to read everything he wrote down. Mainly because what he writes is true.

The worst of me.

He saw the worst of me.

Maybe that is why he chose to forget me now?

'. . . in 80 per cent of cases . . . the person with delusion . . . wanted to leave . . .'

I just didn't think if he did it would be quite like this.

Most days I feel as though someone has punched me in the chest. Like a horse has kicked me flat. My heart literally aching. It is painful for Jesse and Mabel to witness. The WhatsApp missives fly back and forth. Everyone is struggling as we are told not to contradict Jacob's delusion. To play along with it. But still my paranoia grows. I start to notice that other people's partners seem to be sitting in on therapy sessions. I discover that there are workshops to help family communicate better with their injured relatives, and no one invites me.

I start to feel more and more invisible.

It's hard for everyone.

It's no one's fault.

They are hurting for me too.

One day Josh, comments that it is

'Fucking ridiculous . . .' and it is almost a relief to see him stand up for me. To see him want to tell Jacob that his thinking is

'Fucking crap . . . fucking shit.'

Sometimes Jacob drifts. They tweak his antipsychotic medication. He can be fluent, listening and then stray off topic. The EEG is put back on again. Dr M, a lovely Irish consultant who we first met in MITU, is working in rehab for a bit. They think Jacob might be having seizures again. To visiting friends he starts to confess that he has a lot on his mind. One day he makes me cry when, for the first time, he says—

'It's sad I don't know you.'

And I see he genuinely means it.

'Yes, it is, Jacob.'

I buy his love with cake.

Or obscure jokes.

One day I wheel past him in a stray wheelchair and hand him a carrot. Then leave. He peers after me, curious. I do anything just to provoke a reaction. Just for him not to ignore me.

I am in a meeting on *The Split*, and my cellphone rings. It's Jacob's number. I pick up.

'Jacob?'

'Hi,' says the stilted voice back.

In the background I hear a voice—

'Tell your wife what you are doing?'

'I'm calling you. I'm having a therapy session,' Jacob says.

'That's good, Jacob. I'm glad.' I smile, a boardroom of faces looking back at me.

'Yes,' he says.

'Who are you talking to Jacob?' the voice says in the background.

Jacob goes silent. I recognise the voice as Dr T. Dr T has had the genius idea to get Jacob to call me. In some cases, it works for the deluded person to speak to his or her 'imposter' on the phone. Sometimes the voice is recognised, in a way the person is denied. It is also suggested that you start talking to the person, loudly, before you come into the room. Dr T thinks he is trying something new, but I'm familiar with the theory because I have Googled it.

Jacob is getting nicer, looking out for my arrival, even smiling as I lay a trail of crumbs for him in the hope that he will come back to me. One day he puts his arm around me. We hug awkwardly, both pretending that he has finally worked out it is me, even though we both know we are lying.

'Jacob?' the voice in the background prompts again.

'I don't know,' Jacob replies.

He hangs up.

I go back to my meeting, quiet humiliation stinging.

Back to the pages of whatever script I am editing, and I say,

'Cut . . . Can we cut this bit?'

Easter: we go to Puglia, with my mum, Huw and Sophie and the boys. Our house is perched on the edge of Ostuni, the white city, overlooking the Adriatic. The weather is bright, warm, with a chill in the afternoon. Swifts dive-bomb the pool and the children play doubles on the tennis court Jacob has built, far back on a piece of land, behind the olive trees. We stuff mini cream eggs into the holes that pockmark the stone walls of our *trullo* for the kids to find. In the evening, you can climb onto the roof and look out over the green olive landscape, dotted with other half-hidden *trulli* like ours. It is beautiful. But I am restless.

I can't sleep again. Sophie and Huw sometimes come and sit with me when it's 3 a.m., and I've been scrolling on my iPhone or watching Netflix in the living room, where the internet is better, my face illuminated, and the murmur of the TV has woken them up. The ache in my chest is getting worse. I am stressed and tired and I cry a lot, not able to see how the future will be, frightened of this next Act. They comfort and hold my hand. My mum strokes my back as I sit in the sun. But I have a growing sense of dread, that something is not right. The throb grows louder, more painful in my chest.

I promise to go to see my GP, and mentally tell myself off for the screening letters I have missed. A few weeks before Jacob collapsed, he had slid another letter under my nose.

'Go to the bloody doctor. You've not had a smear in five years.'

I go home, tell my friend Sarah, a director that I have often worked with, that there is this ache in my chest. It might be indigestion. I have eaten a lot of pasta. And ice cream. And Diet Coke. And months of coffee and chocolate. Plus, the constant driving, back and forth, a journey I can now do in my sleep. I am wondering if it has been the seat belt rubbing. She tells me to book a breast check-up at the St John and Elizabeth.

'You're in and out in a few minutes . . . Then you don't have to think about it again.'

I book an appointment. Despite the fact that I look bloated and wired, I convince myself that, in the photos of me with Mabel, Ruby and Deb on a cold spring day, I look surprisingly well. My cheeks are flushed. I even look happy. Dorcas asks if I want her to come with me, but I reassure her.

'I'll be in and out. It'll be nothing.'

Dr P is smiling and bouncy like Tigger. He wears pointed boots and suits with bold linings and has an Avengers badge on his lapel. I lie on the paper-lined couch. He examines me, and quickly sends me down for a mammogram. As I squeeze and press my left breast into the flat iron of Perspex, aided by a rubber-gloved nurse, I think two things. 1) – This is surprisingly difficult and humiliating. 2) – Whoever designed this machine must have been a man. It takes forever and they do a biopsy there and then, puncturing my skin with a needle and extracting a thin slither of flesh. I watch my breast up on a screen. Black-and-white shadowy imaging, not unlike Jacob's MRI, the breast not unlike the lobes of his brain.

I go back up and Dr P smiles, and then takes my hand.

'I am 99 per cent sure your results are going to come back positive for breast cancer.'

Fuck . . . Fuck . . .

I stare back at him.

Fuck . . .

I wonder why Avengers? I think.

7

Superheroes come in many forms.

This is the mantra that will go round and round in my head. Keeping time with the steady intermittent electronic peeps of the MRI, like a bad 1970s sci-fi. It reminds me of the Smash ad I used to love as a kid, where metal-headed aliens scoffed at how we earthlings made mashed potato. As I slowly glide through the tubular machine, the theme tune is humming in my head.

'For mash get Smash . . .'

I watched a lot of TV as a kid. Before it was bad, or thought to drain your brain, it was the electronic babysitter that kept us happy. *The Tomorrow People*, *The Banana Splits*, *Poldark*, the original *Doctor Who*, the Tom Baker years, *The Liver Birds*, *The Two Ronnies*, *Morecambe and Wise*, *The Generation Game*. There's not a theme tune that I can't sing, that Huw and Dorcas won't recognise.

'Are you dancing . . . Are you asking? Yeah, I'm asking . . . Then I'm dancing.'

I once wrote to *Jim'll Fix It* and asked if he could 'fix it' for me to be on *The Liver Birds*. He never did.
I count my blessings.
The voice through my headphones calmly interrupts as the clanging momentarily stops—
The Clangers . . . That's one I missed.

'OK, and the next one will be in three minutes.'

I have asked them to break my scan down into chunks. To talk to me. Talk me down. It has taken an hour and half a Valium to get me in here. Dorcas is waiting for me outside, and the radiographer's assistant almost had to unpeel my fingers from her before bringing me in. It's a simple process. I lie on my front, my breasts hanging in two Perspex boxes, which is weird but maybe in a certain light could classify as kinky. A mirror reflects the image of the radiographer and the assistant in the control room, heads down, eyes grazing over the images coming through, speaking to me over the two-way radio, their voices reassuring me through the headphones I am wearing.

Last week I lay in a bone scanner, a flat metal plate a centimetre above my face, but no wider than your average TV. My mother is holding my hand. If I turn a little to my left, while trying not to move my spine, because they need to get my skeleton in perfect shot, I can see her smiling. It's a little like being inside a sandwich toaster. Yet I cry. Like I have never cried before. Weeping like a child, calling out for my mother until she grips my fingers, whispers reassurances to me.

'It's alright, I'm here.'

Machinery is my Achilles heel. The clangs. The peeps. The 'suck' in suctioning. The wheeling out and wheeling in. I have struggled with all of these while I've watched Jacob, and now it's happening to me. My children are used to this phobia. Mabel, leaning in, talking me down, when we stop momentarily in a lift. Jesse, reassuring me as the train dips down into the underground. Once Jacob inadvertently locked me in our car, as he ran into the house to take a phone call. I could see him happily chatting, standing in the living room bay window, phone pressed to his ear, whilst I sat in our drive, trying to call out to the passing traffic of neighbours through the grates of the air conditioning, for someone to set me free.

'So . . . so dramatic . . .' Jacob ribbed me about it for a week.

I am one of life's natural claustrophobics. I can feel claustrophobic in cars. In planes. In lifts. Driving through the Blackwall Tunnel can trigger ridiculous irrational fears, a sense of time slowing and life draining. The feeling of being suspended with no way out. I once had to leave a hairdresser's because sitting still in the chair brought on such a swell of panic. I left with half a haircut, my penance, worn for a week until I could go back and get the other half trimmed.

It makes me think of all the camera tests I have watched actors have to do. Standing in costume against a portion of a set, they are quietly scrutinised, imprisoned under the gaze of various heads of departments discussing what does and doesn't work, and they bear it with such quiet, remote dignity. But then they are in a role. I am playing myself.

I am pathetic. I am a pussy.

'Jacob has endured a thousand of these,' I tell myself.

But still the tears smart, I cry for a God I neither trust nor even think exists. The pulse of the radioactive currents washing over me.

It's like being buried alive.

And once again proves my point.

To opt for cremation. No lying in this box thing.

'Well done, Abi. The next one will be five minutes.'

153

'Seriously . . . So, so dramatic' I hear Jacob's voice in my ear.

I have to consider the possibility I am going to die. They have found a six-centimetre tumour in my left breast, with tendrils that have spread to fourteen centimetres. The good news is that it's moved out rather than in and a removal and biopsy of three nodes reveal it hasn't spread into my lymph nodes. I'm going to lose my breast plus nipple. But still, this seems a win. If they can keep me alive. It's Triple Negative Cancer, meaning it doesn't have the typical receptors oestrogen, progesterone and HER2 protein, so hormone treatment and the targeted cancer drug Herceptin won't work. It's aggressive and relatively rare, affecting 15 per cent of breast cancer patients. Fast growing. Stage 3, grade 3. I chant these three statements. My second new mantra. A little morbid. But this is my kind of Buddhism. Facts. Science. A course of action. Jacob would approve. Twenty weeks of chemo, once every two weeks for the first eight, then weekly for the last twelve. Then a month later a mastectomy. And then three weeks after that, four weeks of radiotherapy. I'll be finished by February. It dawns on me that I am catching up with him, we will now both have had chemotherapy. I find myself checking the drugs sheet at the end of his bed, playing pharmaceutical bingo and wanting to shout 'house' whenever I can see one that matches.

It's June. Jacob has been in hospital for a year.

And the scans do have a certain kind of mawkish beauty. Both mine and Jacob's. The tumour in my breast, marked up as a black hole puncturing the white strata of tissue and skin. The right and left lobe of Jacob's brain, the vivid darkening around the hippocampus which plays an important role in the consolidation of short- and long-term memory, like some long-forgotten galaxy yet to be reached. Our bodies writ large on computer and CT screen, our own spinning universes. Galaxies within. Miraculous structures, to be mulled over, assessed, considered by consultants and radiographers and oncologists.

'The Numbskulls.' *The Beano. Whizzer and Chips.*

My brain freefalls, memories of my childhood dissolving and reappearing.

'The Bash Street Kids.'

My sister was always the cheerleader of 'fun'. She would rally me and my brother Huw into new adventures on the long summer holidays spent at my grandparents' in Cardiff. The pebbledash of their 1930s suburban semi melds with day trips to Barry Island and knickerbocker glories and welsh cakes, pink sausages and fat chips. One year, Dorcas is chief editor of the 'Cardiff Gazette' in charge of recipes and crosswords, my brother and I in charge of . . . who can remember what . . . comic strips? Another wet summer, an entire mini fairground was built out of straws and cotton reels. And plate gardens, digging earth and piling it onto my grandma's best china and then creating ornate paths out of pieces of pebbledash, flowerbeds out of petals and ponds out of Quality Street wrappers.

They hold me through this, my brother and sister, capes well hidden, but still they are part of the growing band of Avengers, walking alongside the oncologists and surgeons and nurses who save me.

Superheroes come in many forms. Superheroes come in many forms.

Sitting with them in the expensive coffee shop across

from the St John & Elizabeth, where my cancer result has just been confirmed, they rally, like dutiful henchmen, either side of me. Asking Dr P the right questions, as I barely take it in, life swirling in a blur. I am unable to take my eyes off Dr P's feet.

'Is he wearing cowboy boots?'

He is.

They buy me coffee and stroke my hand, offering that certain kind of sibling love that I observe in Jesse and Mabel. Wordless, deep-rooted in years of lives lived in parallel, comforting, home. I am lucky. So lucky. I lean into my brother, at once out of puff. The bonds of blood, love and shared history holding me up. I'm not sure if I can do this. But do this I will. Or they will, pulling me along, like they did when we were kids.

But I'm scared.

I'm so fucking scared.

'OK Abi, you're doing really well. The next one will be eight minutes.'

Clang . . . clang . . . clang . . .

The trips to buy comics from the corner shop at the end of St Ina Road, close to my grandparents' street. The memories coming more vividly now. Black jacks, fruit salads and walnut whips in the days when you could get everything for 10p including a packet of crisps.

'It must be the Valium,' I think.

And comics, *Misty*, *Bunty*, *Tammy*, graduating up to *Jackie* and *Just Seventeen* to be read and re-read, back in my grandparents' single guest bedroom, chewing sweets. The summers that I have earmarked as my childhood, before real life came and interrupted it.

There is always one moment in childhood when the door opens and lets the future in.

Graham Greene . . . this time . . .

I think of my own children.

Is this it? The moment when their childhood is broken?

Their father collapses. And now this?

We're one man down already.

Seriously?

The panic is kicking in . . .

Shit . . . Shit . . .

'OK, two more minutes. The next one is coming in two minutes.'

I'm losing it.

'Oh.'

This is Jacob's reaction to my diagnosis.

I am sitting facing him, in his cramped bay. He is perched in a plastic, wooden-armed chair, his wheely tray balanced with the usual chaotic skyline of juices, iPad and whatever else can fit in an NHS-issue cardboard kidney dish.

'That's not good.' Jacob furrows his brows.

'You think? No shit?' but I don't say this.

'No. But the good news is, you'll still have lots of people to visit you and bring you books. And I'll come in, in between.'

'In between – what?'

'My treatments. Chemotherapy.'

'That's not good.'

'No,' I reply.

And then he makes a face, which looks a lot like really bad acting, crying but without tears. It becomes Jacob's way to show me he is sad, even though I am not entirely sure he knows why.

'Can we still go to Carluccio's?'

I nod.

He resumes watching whatever he's watching on Netflix.

'This is peculiar,' I think.

I know I should say something wise about cancer. I have no doubt there is much that is profound to be found in it. But right now, in the film from the book of this, this bit, it's too much—

'It's doing the same thing.' My internal editor chips in, in the imaginary meeting, about the film adapted from the book, re my cancer.

'First thing to go. It's just . . . honestly . . . it's boring.'

'Yeah . . . Agreed . . . And we've already got the coma bit.'

And it is, it's mainly boring. Or as Dr P gleefully smiles and says—

'This is going to be a massive inconvenience.'

A massive inconvenience.

Boring and a massive inconvenience.

But it's not without its . . . scratch . . . gifts.

I tell myself that chemotherapy will be an opportunity to catch up on the many box sets I've missed. My first cycle – I think why not crack the opening eight episodes of *Game of Thrones*? Amazing. But after I do, I will find at any point in the future I can't hear the theme tune without feeling sick. And lying on the sofa all day reveals two things. 1) – The demographic of daytime television

watchers cares about donkey sanctuaries and accident insurance. Or so the algorithm that is programming thinks.
2) – *The Pioneer Woman* on Food Network is addictive.

I watch a lot of this.

Ree Drummond, aka *Pioneer Woman*, is a vivacious auburn-haired blogger, author, food writer and television personality. She makes a lot of cowboy chilli and grits for Ladd Drummond, her husband, while he's out on the ranch. Google will reveal that the Mercantile, or as she calls it the 'Merc', the quaint restaurant she 'runs' in Oklahoma, serves 6,000 dinners a day and that Ladd, who Ree affectionately calls her 'Marlboro Man', owns 433,000 acres and is one of the largest landowners in the US. My kids now hate cowboy chilli. Note to self . . . Stop Googling so much shit.

People will say to me—'Well, no wonder he can't recognise you. Without your hair you look so different.'
He being Jacob. And they being random well-meaning people, but they do have a point. I do look different when my hair is shaved off, a few days before my first chemo. Like an oversized, bloated baby, the wisps around my neck only adding to the feeling that I am an extra in *Quadrophenia*. Or a de-wigged witch in Roald Dahl's *The Witches*. Still, I will take selfies in the naïve belief I am rocking it. And I make a new discovery. Jacob will insist that even the selfies I take are not Abi Morgan. Neither are any photos from the past recognised as Abi Morgan. It seems this 'imposter' has been around longer than either of us thought.

My fascination grows with what she actually looks like, the Abi Morgan who has abandoned ship. We know that

that Abi Morgan has long dark hair and blue eyes, but what of her nose, the shape of her face? I wonder whose face he has blended her with, from which file in the upended cabinet that is now his brain, he has taken her from.

In my mind I map out a photofit of her, playing bad detective again. The irony is that it is he who has always been better suited to this physical shapeshifting. The cubby holes on the melamine notice board above his desk still filled with the strange pairs of glasses, or tiepins, or other character accessories poached from whatever backstage props table or film he had been working on.

It is he who loved to source costumes, arriving home one day with gangster suits and mobster moll dresses for himself and me and the kids. Dragging us on a wet night to a backwater of East London, to throw fake custard pies and dance at Fat Sam's café in an immersive Secret Cinema staging of *Bugsy Malone*. The four of us slip sliding across the floor of some beautiful 1930s art deco cinema in plastic raincoats, hair plastered to our heads, covered in shaving-foam pie, eating meatballs and drinking Singapore Gin Slings, giddy, flushed yet alive.

The fun . . . the memories of the fun, will keep me going, however much they sting.

They will remind me.

I did exist.

I can exist.

I will exist a little time more.

I will also learn that my children will be even more miraculous than they have already been. I mentally make a note to earmark an account to pay for the therapy that they will inevitably need. They will love me, and hold me, and yawn when I try and pull the cancer card. And later, when I have no left breast, they will make jokes, Mabel in particular, that they are looking for something—

'Shit, Mum . . . Where's your boob gone?'

I will come to hate the 'boob' that will fill the gap where my breast once lay. Two pounds of rubber and silicone that I have been fitted with in a bra that quite frankly I wouldn't be seen dead in, even by the kind thoughtful nurses. I will pull out and randomly dump that silicone puddle on the hall table as soon as I am home, because it rubs and makes my neck ache. Until Mabel's piano teacher looks at it curiously as he passes it en route to the living room and I will remember to hide it in future. But I will continue to take selfies, on my own or with the dog, but always with one of us wearing it, balanced like a pillbox hat on our head.

I will never be more grateful for the people who love me: Jacqui, my running partner going through her own cancer journey, who was the first person I called the day Jacob collapsed; my mother and my family who are always, always there; Jacob's family who will keep Jacob's visits going when I am too sick to get out of bed; and my friends, who call, text, send flowers and cake, and who are just there. Simply there. Old girlfriends and new, my best male friends, mums from school, neighbours now pals, I lean into. All of them will surround me, try to fill the gaping hole that is Jacob, that is the absence of Jacob, the loss of which will still wake me in the night, like a punch to the heart.

If I am honest, it is not as bad as I thought it was going to be. And in many ways, it is worse. I kick myself for spending so much of life being fearful and am so grateful to Jacob for his fearlessness. In January he would start plotting trips, scratching out places we have visited on a map on the wall. California, Costa Rica, Bangkok, Vancouver. South Africa was planned for the Christmas after he collapsed. I didn't go abroad until I was eighteen, something unimaginable for my kids. Jacob, whilst reticent in a roomful of casting directors or producers, was intrepid when it came to mountains, sea or sand.

In the early days, when the kids were very young, we drove around Sicily, stopping the car to leap off a rock into icy water, or to visit a bar, because it had a great review. In France, coming back on a sleeper from the mountains, with an hour between trains, he would drag us, overloaded rucksacks and ski boots in tow, to some backwater burger bar, because he'd read that all the best jazz musicians and rap artists went there, and the burgers are the best in town. And they were, still are, the best I've ever had. In another life, without Jacob, I would have bought a stale sandwich on a station platform and waited there, nervous I might miss my train. Always, always, I was the nervous one. Always he would reassure me or make me laugh, make me brave. And I am so grateful to him. For pushing me over the edge, of cliffs and zip wires and down mountains and off diving boards and into deep water.

Danger is much more domestic.

It was nestling in my breast.

I will never walk again not knowing how close to the edge of the cliff, life can take you, ordinary life. And that over that cliff, I come to see, is death.

And it is dark.

And endless.

And unknown.

And I don't want it yet.

Not yet.

But it will happen.

One day.

And I hope, when it happens, I will leap with both arms in a swan dive.

As Jacob has taught me.

But still it lingers. Mortality lingers.

'Yeah, but I think you've got all that with Jacob . . . the themes of mortality, life's impermanent nature, can we just cut to the bit when he comes back?'

My internal editor, infuriating, is again chipping in.

It's a feeling I can't shake.

For a long time.

The feeling that life is finite and time is running out.

When I watched my own father die, over five days in a hospital in Manchester a decade before, I kept on telling myself . . .

'Remember this . . . Don't forget this. Do things different . . . Be different . . . You will be different . . . You will remember that life is not a dress rehearsal.'

And then, like childbirth, you do . . . forget.

I become obsessed with Instagram pages of those with cancer and in awe of those who don't get better. Those who will learn to live 'with' or die from this disease that will affect one in two people in a lifetime, all the while blogging. And that even in people's worst moments, body creams and expensive sleep masks sent as 'gifts' by 'fans' are another way of maintaining product placement. Because having cancer is expensive, mentally, physically, practically. And I will buy this shit as a result of what the sick or dying are willing to sell.

That I can be so grateful that it makes my cheeks ache from smiling.

And not just to the people who save me. Dr P, Dr A, my elegant oncologist who looks like she should head up the UN. Not just the nurses who come to my house and pump me with EC chemo and paclitaxel. I turn over their names in my head, worried that these, like anti-NMDA receptor encephalitis, will be misplaced, forgotten by me. Not just the radiologist who will sit with me for an hour during a session which should take ten minutes because I am hyperventilating, terrified of the machine. Of the machine that means I have to hold my breath, so the beam won't get my heart, eyes fixed on the narrow green bar that I must keep perfectly still, viewed through strange goggles propped just above my head and mirroring my breathing.

1 . . . 2 . . . 3 . . .

'That's it, Abi. You can exhale now.'

And I can exhale, let the green bar drop again.

But also grateful to all the others.

The ones who don't know how much they did for me.

One day I watch a neighbour cleaning fox shit off my path.

And that in the end, it will be the little things that will finally pull me back to myself, to knowing who I am. And that some of those little things, that will clang like a magnet, will send shock waves back to Jacob too, wherever he is.

*

I am sitting facing Jacob, trying to tidy his hospital bed. I am on the fourth cycle of my now weekly chemotherapy. I am utterly exhausted, hollowed out.

It is brutal.

It is savage.

And Jacob is not making it easy.

I tidy around him. He is watching as I throw out the half-eaten biscuits and the old orange peel that has accumulated around his bed again. It is July. Nearly his birthday. And this time it will be a birthday that he can attend. He is coming home for his first visit. He is getting stronger, getting better. He can walk up and down the stairs now, still with a slight Frankenstein gait, but he can move, he is healing. He is coming back a little more each day. There is even talk he may be discharged in a few weeks. The muscles visible, calves sinewing once more on his legs.

It's hot. Too hot in this ward where the radiators stay on even in the summer. The guy with the droopy eye has left months ago. Brian is making good progress in a bay in the next ward, his wife Diane tells me. I look ill, more ill than Jacob. Last week, I lay down on Jacob's bed while he was in the gym, and a grumpy nurse passing, mop in hand, stopped at the end of it.

'What are you doing being ill all over the place? What's wrong with you?'

'Sorry. I'm not feeling great,' I reply.

'Well, don't go bringing your illness here.'

Which is valid, though I would argue, if you're ill then what better place to be than hospital.

Jacob's hungry, so we go out. We walk over to Brunswick Square, the sixties modernist shopping centre with the fast-food restaurants whose menus we know by heart. We sit outside and order. Jacob is smiley. A couple of weeks ago he tried to kiss me, amorously. I had brushed it off with a smile, it had been like kissing as a teenager, eager but lacking finesse. But I had eagerly reported it to Dr T, hopeful that this was a breakthrough. He furrowed his brow, clearly concerned, actually more than concerned, almost excited.

'Very good. It's very important you tell me. We're playing around with his antipsychotics so he may do that. We'll take them down a bit.'

And I am back in the playground, feeling like I have just confessed the kiss to friends, only to discover that it has been denied by the giver.

'We're cool, right . . . I mean it didn't mean anything.'

I'm reminded that as much as we are taking care of Jacob, my heart, like my body, is also fragile.

'Fuck you, Dr T. '

But I don't say this.

'Ah right . . . I thought it might be something like that.'

Even so, something is shifting in Jacob. We sit outside Carluccio's, him staring at me, me staring back. Like the odd couple, he with his walker, me bald and bloated, our starters just delivered.

'Your head's flat at the back,' he suddenly observes, words puncturing a now customary silence.

I look up, carefully eating my burrata, not wanting to trigger memories of last summer, that early flicker of Jacob's madness.

'What?'

And just like that, he reaches out a hand, leans across the table, and touches the back of my head gently.

The warmth of his hand surprising me with its familiarity. Jacob used to posit the theory that it was because I had been left too long in my pram as a baby. And somewhere the magnets in Jacob's brain momentarily bang together, sending out a wave of memory.

'Like Abi . . . Abi Morgan.'

Clang . . .

'Yes Jacob, like Abi Morgan.'

I cut my burrata.

I look back at him.

He smiles.

I smile.

Clang . . .

I want to tell Jacob I once counted the moles on his back. And to touch the bubble, a hardened blood blister, in his left earlobe that you can feel if you pinch, the legacy of some long-ago teenage ear piercing, the hole now sealed. And how I know it used to irritate him when I would absently touch it, as he drove, me next to him, listening to music and going nowhere. I want to remind him that I know every inch of his body, as he does mine. Every vulnerability shared, every best featured admired, every physical mishap that has left its imprint on our bodies is known to one another. I want to touch the scar just to the left of my bottom lip and ask him, as I sometimes would on bored and lazy mornings in our kitchen, if he remembered how I got it.

'Apple tree, running in an orchard when you were . . . Eight . . . Nine . . .You were nine.'

'Well done. And this?' I would point to the thin slither of skin on my left index finger, paler than the rest of my finger.

'Bread knife . . . When you were fourteen?'
I want to say,
  'I know you. You know me.'
But I don't. I'm too tired.
Because I have cancer.
I have cancer.
So instead, I say,
  'Do you want a dessert?'

They are worried Jacob could hurt me. In the meeting, the big meeting we have with all Jacob's therapists: psychiatrist, psychologist, neurologists, OTs. D-day is fast approaching.

  'Has he ever seemed aggressive towards you?'

  'No,' I reply.

I recall the student films on YouTube. On Capgras. The bad acting. The scary music. I think in one of them, set in the Victorian era, there is a stabbing scene. Which is also weird and inaccurate, because Capgras wasn't even named until 1923.

  'No. He's never been aggressive towards me.'

And this is true. Jacob is always sweet. As if the very best of him has been left, like a guest sitting alone when everyone else has left the table, quite happy to be the last. There's a warmth and humour that is utterly Jacob, still staring back at me.

  'I don't think he ever would be.'

He is not sitting in on this meeting.

  'There are cases, and that would be my concern.' Dr T again. I give Dr T the eye.

Clearly, we've been watching the same films.

Oh my God. They're not going to let me take him home.

'He's fine. He's fine with me,' I respond firmly.

And it's true.

We've come to a happy compromise.

I buy Jacob cake. And dessert.

He smiles, reluctantly accepting me.

'But I'm not Abi? Abi Morgan?' I ask him.

'No.' Jacob giggles. We have gone out for tea, the week after he touched my head. Dainty sandwiches and scones on a cake stand. The gentle drone of Southampton Row smogs the windows as we eat. This is progress. At least he's replied. I know he does talk to other people. In the weeks before rehab, he once pulled my brother aside.

'You can see she's not Abi Morgan. Can't you?'

My brother treads carefully.

'Well, she seems like my sister, Jacob. I mean, no, she's Abi Morgan to me.'

Usually, Jacob is uncomfortable when I ask him directly. But I've long tired of the Theory A Theory B malarky, dropped weeks ago. I've gone maverick.

'Then why do the kids call me Mum?' I go in again.

Now I just rattle his cage, to see how close he'll come to the bars. Or up for air, from the deep pool of water I sometimes imagine his rocket ship has crashed into.

And he just looks long and hard at me, whilst piling more jam on to a mini scone. Again, this is progress. He's multitasking, it's physically and cognitively challenging, yet he's thinking whilst eating.

'I haven't worked that out yet.'

It's weird.

Jacob's smiling OT tells us that Jacob is going to need care for the rest of his life. Carers to wash and dress him and help him to the toilet.

'Probably twenty-four hours a day.'

And he'll always wear a nappy. And be impotent. It's getting better and better.

'We've seen real progress. But I don't think we've got very far neurologically,' Dr B offers up with a smile.

We're still in this meeting, Jacob's final meeting. His family are also in attendance, sitting in a ring with Jacob's vast team. Ten to fifteen people listening and listening, waiting for their turn to speak, like some self-help group, not entirely sure of what our addiction is.

'Jacob's always going to need prompting on everything.'

We ask questions, discuss Jacob's aftercare. We can apply for help, Brett, Jacob's social worker, reassures us. He's Canadian and feels like he's stepped out of an am-dram production of *High School Musical*, where no one is younger than thirty-five. Katie, Jacob's keyworker, sweet and smiling, is more encouraging.

'He's making real strides.'

I grab at this.

'80 per cent of anti-NMDA encephalitis patients recover fully eventually,' I offer hopefully.

Dr B catches on this—

'Jacob's on the severe end of that 80 per cent.'

There is concern about whether I can cope and for a minute I can't quite see why.

But then I remember I have cancer. Something which I keep forgetting, as if it is the last ingredient on a list, and I am standing in the supermarket as I often do, knowing that there is something missing. And though at the time, I will think I am rocking it, my face is so swollen with steroids that sometimes my skin feels too tight even to open my eyes.

'I mean you still have—'

'. . . Six months of my treatment to go,' I reply.

And in that moment, I do wonder how I am going to do this. Get this man home and better, get my kids to school, get the show I have written made, get myself through cancer.

'I bought a new bed. I'm making his office into his bedroom.'

This throws them off the scent. I need to show them I am competent, that I can do this, that I can take him home. Where he belongs. Because I hold on to this manic belief that if I can get him through the door, down the stairs, into the white . . . white . . . kitchen that we wrestled over . . . that is filled with light . . . and sit him on the bench that he designed . . . that somehow he will know that he is home, and I am me . . . his wife . . . partner . . . wife . . .

I will later read in his final discharge report the following:

'Discharge planning is difficult due to concerns of continuing aggression towards his wife.'

I am oblivious to this.

They make notes and I wonder if this meeting is to reassure us or them. Because we, like Jacob, have become institutionalised, coming into this place day in and day out for over a year now. Working around Jacob's rehab rotas, bagsying visiting times on WhatsApp, politely working around one another, trying to give one another space.

And we are exhausted.

'Did I say I've bought a new bed?'

And as I leave the meeting, I realise how daunting this is.

We are taking home Jacob, but not Jacob.

A stranger who is strange and yet not a stranger at all.

And I'm scared.

I'm really scared.

In the chapel downstairs, they hold a singing group for patients that your OT encourages you to join. I read somewhere auditory memory may be the last thing to die because it is the first thing learnt. We sing to our babies, even before they are born. A way to express in music what we cannot say in words. In the end we all vie to take you, the experience is so sweet and moving. A hearty and eminently impressive choirmistress leads this ragbag of patients, old and young, bashing away on a piano, and jumping up and down like a tamer Victoria Wood. You have developed a love of Beatles songs, and she is happy to oblige. You sit, tuneless, yet utterly absorbed, still refusing to talk to anyone, yet singing your heart out. A young man, in his thirties, thickset, gait like a child, his trainers split, stands in the middle of the group crying. I can hear his parents, in to visit, calling out for him, and then quietly sinking down in their seats at the back, when he waves at them not to interrupt. I find it distracting and yet, looking back at you, you do not waver from your song.

Suddenly
I'm not half the man I used to be . . .
And I don't know if I can bear this.
I don't know how to do this.
Dig deep.
Dig . . .
Deep.

Rewind.

We are on holiday. Canada. A magical trip. A week on a houseboat. White water rafting in Whistler. A night on a ranch. The kids are little – eight and ten. For the last week, we fly to Vancouver Island, on a model-size seaplane that takes us up and over the vast lakes, the logging route for vast Douglas firs and cedars floated down the West Coast, when Vancouver was the heart of the timber industry in the nineteenth century. A last week of surfing and whale watching in tiny tugboats with drunken captains, stopping off at the crab shacks and restaurants that run along the road to Tofino bay. One night, we ride on our bicycles along the long winding road to a restaurant. By the time we leave to head back, it's dark. The bikes have no lights. There are no taxis for miles and no other way to get home.

By the main road, there is a narrow slipway, edged by water. It is completely dark, not a star in the sky. To the right, the streak of cars is intermittent, but we can only hope their lights will catch us like deer, caught mid-glare.

'Let's do this.'

The mantra you punched out when I know you are scared.

Whistling over the canopy of trees, thousands of feet above the air in Costa Rica, on zip wires as thin as linguine and you'd shout—

'Open your eyes. You'll miss the view.'

Diving deep in the waters of Thailand, and Greece, with children still trying to learn to balance their breathing and oxygen tanks.

Perched on the back of motorcycle taxis, through the heat of Bangkok, dipping in and out of traffic, with toddlers perched on our laps.

And now this, almost tame in comparison, a bike ride. And yet, it is silent, and there are woods, endless and menacing. Yet you lead us, on crappy bikes, through the starless night. My bike is ancient and will only brake if peddled backwards. I can't see where my feet start and the pedals end. We have been warned not to stay out late, and to be aware of bears. And I have watched *Grizzly Man*. The kids are scared, so you sing, calling out to us inter-mittently—

'Jesse . . . ?'

'I'm here . . .'

'Well done, buddy . . . Mabes . . . ?'

'Here . . . Daddy . . .'

'Abi?'

I'm far behind . . .

'I'm OK.'

Occasionally, the light from a car grazes our faces, skirting too close. But we are too far to go back and too near to give up now.

It is the darkest night. And when we make it home on that cycle ride through the blackest of black, you will capture our laughing relief and flushed faces on your iPhone. The flash catching our pupils, glinting with red eye.

And I will find that photo on my nightly scrolls, searching, searching for something, anything to hold on to. I will find it, and I will treasure it, and remind myself you have always taken us by the hand, and pulled us on, navigated us through the best adventures, the scariest moments.

So, this is the least I can do.

All that I can do.

The only thing to do.

Half the man you used to be . . .

To lead you back.

8

August: we have broken Jacob out of hospital, even though his official discharge is not until September. But the day release has evolved into weekends and we have convinced the doctors he is ready to come home. You will have spent 443 days in hospital in the end. The OTs ask for a video of our house, and I move slowly up the drive, through the front door and into hallway and then living room, working my way up and down like some estate agent, trying to sell a dive, holding up my iPhone filming it all. Apologies for scuffs on the wall, and promises to add additional railing, are the soundtrack that underscores my wobbly camera angles.

We live in Crouch End, which Wikipedia tells me is derived from Middle English. A crouch means 'end', a border, outside of the parish influence, a five-mile-square pocket of North London to the west of Haringey, teeming with coffee shops, actors and young mums. In my mid-twenties, I house-sat for the daughter of my mum's best friend, the writer. Then the best thing about it was an amply stocked Budgens. Now it has two cinemas, Gail's and a good hardware shop. In truth, we live on the borders, Stroud Green if you really want to nail it, equal distance to Finsbury Park, but in Stroud Green you get more bang for your buck. For a few years I had an office in the magnificent if faded Hornsey Town Hall, location for *The Hour*, a show I wrote, set in a fifties newsroom. It was a very happy period in my life. I would amend a scene and the following day that same scene would be shot at the end of my corridor. And best of all, I could walk home in time to give the kids a bath.

I film rooms and places where I realise later Jacob's therapists do not need to go. We have knocked and extended and pushed this house into shape over time; it's grown with the children. Each movie made was another floor renovated or pulled apart.

Our kitchen is *The Iron Lady* wing.

Our bedroom? Thank you, *Suffragette*.

The down payment, a show I wrote for HBO about the Boxing Day tsunami.

Blood money. Other people's lives have inspired me.

And yet filming my own life, my own world, I am nervous, as if I have something to prove. Trying to bring back a partner who no longer remembers you is a crushingly humiliating business. My fear is that I am Kathy Bates in my own version of *Misery*. A quietly psychotic stalker who has persuaded the object of her fandom to stay. I have mental images of chaining Jacob to the bed. I have finally captured Jacob, Jacob, so strong-willed and independent, now so dependent on me. Have I metaphorically kneecapped him into submission with my cake and trips to the cinema and park? I blame myself – still. It is a pointless exercise, but on the nights I cannot sleep, I play detective, working my way back through our past. What foot did I put wrong? People will ask me if I ever question why this has happened to us and I always reply—

'Why not?'

But in truth, it is the question that I turn over again and again in my mind. It's not as if I have not imagined this, this world falling apart. I have a vivid memory of driving home one day, months before Jacob collapsed. I know the exact place on my route when a thought came to mind as I swung a left into our road.

'If Jacob died tomorrow, what would I do?'

By the time I am through our front door, I have imagined the very worst things happening to him, and a whole new life for myself. It's not unpleasant. I am the brave widow. The travelling, the independence, the new romance. Later, it will seem like another mark of carelessness, that I dared to dream, dared to fantasise about a nightmare that was not all bad. Did I will this upon us, upon him? For he is halfway between being back and not being back. There are days when I look on quietly appalled and want to scream,

'Can't you see, you've sent back his ghost.'

Later, much later, Jesse will admit that he thinks the hospital have sent Jacob home too early. On bad days, we quietly rage, whispering between the three of us, Mabel, Jesse and me, the very worst nicknames for this Jacob – Smart Boy, Rain Man, this 'half-dead dad', one particular shameful phrase I coin.

Is it shameful? Or does shame lie with the cruelty of medicine that works so hard to save a life, yet gives no promise of actually bringing the person back? When the front door closes, and Jacob is finally here, I am reminded of when we first brought Jesse home. Jacob and I both staring at him, exquisite in his Moses basket, neither of us quite knowing what to do with this little bundle of flesh and hopeful dreams, coming with no receipt or option of a refund. We were both so eager to lay him on the bed, we slipped and found ourselves both holding the same handle of the Moses basket, and Jesse rolled out of it, days old, and landed in the fireplace. For weeks after, we kept checking him, just as we did in the immediate aftermath, anxiously brushing dust off his tiny face and laying him carefully back on the sheepskin. Looking at Jacob, sitting on the side of his bed, blankly staring at the wall, the same slow and seeping dread pervades. Can we do this? Worse is the feeling,

'Shit – he's back for good.'

I show Jacob the film of our house before he leaves the hospital, perched on the edge of his hospital bed, sitting close to him, as he now allows me, having declared me, in a new but very recent move, 'a friend'. I have morphed from being someone 'state appointed', to someone kindly, who seems to have a slightly uncomfortable affection for him. A little like a parishioner who cooks for the vicar, or a groupie who at last gets to hang out with the band. Jacob's life now packed up into plastic Waitrose and Ikea bags around his hospital bed, we finally prepare to ship him out. I point out where I have changed things – a new chair, a moved table, more pictures on the wall. He looks blankly, nodding occasionally when there is a familiar landmark, an orange bench, the yellow front door. We mulled over that colour for weeks, the wood painted and repainted, different shades mixed and remixed at our local B&Q, Jacob returning each time with a new pot until finally we fixed on the perfect sunflower yellow.

I have transformed Jacob's office into a bedroom of sorts. The expensive pull-down bed is long gone, replaced with a single bed. Lights have been rewired and moved to frame the grey felt headboard. Side tables moved in. A place for his pee bottles and an Alexa he will never learn to use. The first time Jacob sleeps, the dog curls up on the pillow by his head, refusing to move, lying as if on guard, while Jacob snores.

On the walls I have hung a small gallery of pictures and photographs I hope will mean something to him. Another roadmap spread out as if on the bonnet of a car, trying to trigger something, a flicker of a past, that will lead him back. A flow chart of rap names framed and picked up only weeks before he got ill. A poster from *Oslo*, the last play he performed in, the January before his collapse. Recent photos taken in the July just gone, on his birthday, the birthday we never believed he would make. He is smiling, a little bewildered as we look to him to cut the lemon drizzle cake I have made. A haphazard leaning tower of sponge and over-zested whipped cream. His mother, in pale blue shirt smiling next to him, beautiful against the orange bench.

More photos of family, people who he knows and loves. And just in the corner of one picture of Mabel and her cousin Ruby, smiling on a beach in May, there is the edge of my face. Only just visible, almost as if I am afraid he will reject it if I am in shot. Next to it, is a framed page of lyrics, of 'our song', something I gave him a couple of Christmases past. He later told me it was the wrong song. We argued. I hung it anyway. Above it, a clock, which he peers at every morning when I wake him, part of the constant prompting that they will talk about at the hospital in the days before we leave. Jacob will lie waiting for me to wake him and when I do, his eyes spring open ready to start his day.

From this room, Jacob used to run our life, as if captaining the Starship Enterprise. Booking flights, moving money, emailing teachers and organising our diaries, marrying school and work schedules with the enjoyment of a man who marvelled over a difficult Sudoku. The football matches and hockey games, with Jacob always on the touchline. The parties and bar mitzvahs that seemed to come in a frenzy as the kids hit early teens. Jacob volunteering to drive carloads of young boys, dressed up and aftershave on, for the sheer pleasure of listening to the babble of their conversation, sharing in their happiness and excitement, delighted to be part of their team for the last moments before their young adulthood kicked him out. The Friday morning coffees with his gang of school mums – Maria, Philippa, Denise and Lisa K – names and appointments would flash up on my laptop when I would be mid-storyline meeting or script conference. The dentist appointments, visits to the doctor, the monthly injection for his MS at Queen Square. I took comfort from these, the quiet pings and whooshes that emanated from the reminders and send alerts. They told me life was alright, he was on it, all was OK.

On the desk by his bed, his Apple computer sits, dormant and gathering dust. The red chair, expensive and good for his back, which becomes a table on which to balance the plastic gloves and foot creams, the bric-a-brac of this new life. Sitting on the stairs, outside his room at night, I listen to Jacob talking in his sleep, earwigging the way I used to on the snatches of phone calls to agents or some buddy.

Now I listen to the one-sided conversations that permeate Jacob's sleep. In his dreams, he is perfectly coherent, conversing as he did before. In his dreams, there is no bewilderment, no blank stare. In his dreams he is himself again.

'Babe, do you know where I've left the keys?'

'It's OK . . . I've found them . . .'

'No . . . No . . . let's go straight there. We can pick up Chick'n'Sours.'

Slithers of familiar dialogue, plucked from our past, that I wordlessly respond to, a silent player, perched on the stairs. Like familiar recordings of another life that we lived together. Driving in the car, to whatever medical appointment I take him to in those early weeks, Jacob sits next to me, his eyes closed, yet his hand swims, clawing the air. Shaking the hand of an imaginary friend, an audience member, congratulating him after a first night.

'It's good, man . . . It's good to see you.'

'Glad you enjoyed it.'

'It's a wicked play.'

Other times, it is an imaginary glass, raised to his lips.

'That's so good . . . It's really smoky . . .'

In his mind it is an Old Fashioned, his favourite drink. These visual hallucinations come and go. The doctors do not know if they are some kind of seizure or whether he is simply dreaming.

He walks like a toddler now, straight-backed, palms flat by his side, shuffling between the TV and bathroom, re-orientating himself, fingers grazing the walls, gripping the glass bannister that takes him from kitchen to the upstairs hallway. A constant trip hazard, he moves with one of us always behind him, gently pushing him on, pushing him to bed or into the living room.

On one of his first visits back, I find him lying on our bed, in our room, on the top floor, the dog once more beside him, Mabel to his right. He smiles, almost provocatively, on me finding him, spread-eagled and patting the dog, as if he has never left. But that is the only time. As if he knows now that he must stay in his quarters, he rarely steps beyond the first floor. The first night he's home, I lie alone, relieved that I no longer need to imagine him in the sticky, sweltering ward, where the lights were always bright, and someone was always shouting wildly from a distant bed. But still, in this room, 'our' room, where the racks of the clothes are hanging in his closet, no longer fitting the man, I realise we will never sleep together again.

As I come out of the shower every day, I see the squashed layers of jackets and cargo pants, sweatshirts and Hawaiian prints that he loved. A burgundy bomber jacket, worn on a cold weekend in Dublin, where we drank Guinness and wandered the streets aimless and happy. A crazy pink shirt, worn one New Year's Eve on a beach in Costa Rica, as we danced and watched fireworks light up the bay. Jumpers, pulled on during cold Sundays and lazy weekends, frayed and moth eaten but still loved. A tuxedo brought out for rare awards nights and weddings, a stain still on the collar from a candle dripping wax. And the shoes.

Trainers of every colour. Faded suede boots already gathering dust. Plastic dive shoes worn on a trip to Thailand. Pale cream lace-ups never worn, a rash purchase, hurriedly pushed to the back of the rack. On a shelf, a tower of 20ps and pound coins, pulled out of pockets with plans to cash them in one day. Bowls of paracetamol, and nail cutters, his 'wedding' ring, removed, like the chain around his neck, the day he was admitted into hospital, now resting in a soap dish by the basin. The trail of domestic DNA littering our bedroom, that I step around, like a beachcomber, jumping rock pools.

If Jacob had died, I could have bundled these up, with a sense of ritual, delivered them to the doorstep of Marie Curie or Mind. Instead, they hang like costumes from numerous parts, waiting for a performance that will never begin.

'So . . . so dramatic . . .'

Your voice once more in my head.

You're right, but these are dramatic times. But more than this, they are lonely and more, they are boring. No one told me how boring loss is.

At night, I close my eyes, and sometimes I lay a pillow on top of my chest, just wanting, needing, to feel the weight of something, someone, you, again. And in the morning, I go downstairs, wake you up, get you dressed, steer you down to breakfast. Your crooked left hand, fingers bent and taut where nerves have been irrevocably damaged, means it is impossible for you to pull on your clothes, tie your shoes, raise a fork to your mouth. On the first night, the carer we have hired, a nervous boy from southern Italy, with crazy hair, looks at me mournfully and admits this is his first job. Hands shaking as I talk him through the diaper changes, and routine, I see we are as scared as one another. He doesn't come back for a second night.

At the hospital they reassure us that Jacob will qualify for carers, but it becomes apparent that not only is the system slow but it is designed to fail. By October, and despite the obvious, we qualify for nothing. The criteria of needs are so narrow that if he can breathe on his own, we tip into being means tested, and it doesn't take a lot of funds to be disqualified. I do the maths. Twenty-four-hour care will bankrupt us. Five days a week care, 8 a.m.–6 p.m., is just about possible. Plus, the rotation of weekly therapists Jacob will need. Yearly, it's the cost of a small flat in Walthamstow. I call my agent, juggle finances, and ask her to find me a Hollywood gig.

I add this to my gratitude list, that if I push myself hard, we can just about scrape through. But it will take all our savings and will regularly clean us out financially. And long term, something will have to be sold. I lie in bed, late into the night, totting up numbers and moving money in my head as if trying to solve one of those sliding puzzle squares of a cartoon dog, or the like, that you get in a cracker. And however many times I push and slide things around, the nose or tail is still always out. In truth it is the work, the ability and joy of creating and writing, that will be another golden thread that will pull me through. I sign the studio contract, thankful for my agent, and hire more care.

Daniel arrives first; kind and brilliant, he runs the choir at his church every Sunday. Amina, beautiful, neuropsychology student, lives with eight others in Turnpike Lane. We fumble to find our way together, with a patchwork of therapists who come and go. Physios, an OT, speech and language therapist, neuropsychologist, all working towards waking you up, pushing you forward, getting you back. The cocktail of drugs, to cheer you up, calm you down, stop seizures, start cognition, grease the cogs in your body and brain, are pushed from a blister pack twice a day and into your mouth.

There are days when you crash and days where your eyes silently follow me as I make coffee, go about my day. At night, I put you to bed. One day you notice a sweater I am wearing.

'I bought that for Abi,' you say.

It is the colour of pistachios.

'Yes – Christmas before last,' I reply.

'You'll stretch it.'

'Should I take it off?' I offer.

'Yes – that's probably a good idea,' you reply.

In our hallway, there is a large mirror, and occasionally when I have propped you up against the wall and am searching for your coat on a hook, I see you staring at yourself, taking in your own reflection.

'Who's that?' I ask.

You silently stare back at yourself, with obvious disappointment.

'I don't know.'

'You're Jacob,' I reply.

And you do this thing you used to do before we'd go out, when you were checking the line of a jacket, or wanting to raise yourself an inch above your five foot nine, you puff your chest and raise your head a little, readying yourself.

'Don't you look handsome?' I say.

And you nod, humouring me, like a little boy.

I have come to see that you are as much a stranger to yourself as I am to you.

*

Bonnie-Kate, the neuropsychologist we have found, and who comes weekly to our house and sits in our kitchen, talks of PTSD, and I am reminded of the days in the hospital you sat bolt upright, your face twitching, brain storming with electricity. I reassure myself that your brain scans look the same in September as they did in the early months until Liz, your inspiring Australian speech therapist, calmly tells me that the blank smile, and blank mind, is not just your brain trying to repair.

It's permanent.

Irreparable.

Brain damage.

The house is full, constantly full, so that even the dog retreats to his post on the sofa, keeping guard, eyeing suspiciously the traffic in and out of the house. Physiotherapists, speech and language therapists, OTs, neuropsychologists, carers. A constant industry, all focused on you. Tash, brilliant and working in music, finds you a choir to join.

One day someone has put you in a mysterious T-shirt, too small, with your belly poking out underneath, like some teen at a Jonas Brothers concert. It is printed with the words *If Things Get Better with Age, I Am Approaching Magnificence.* You barely look up from shovelling cornflakes in your mouth, in a bowl piled high, slopping milk, oblivious. This is a man who would spend hours sourcing a cool T-shirt or expensive fraying sweatshirt. I tell myself those were just vanities, and it doesn't matter. Still, I find myself sitting in our downstairs loo, stuffing my hand in my mouth, trying not to scream.

Another day, Amina has got you up and you are doing

Zumba in the living room. This is a low point, watching you miserably shuffling back and forth to Gloria Estefan and *Rhythm Is Gonna Get You* in our living room. You are a beautiful dancer, an amazing dancer, reduced to this, like an old-age pensioner doing morning exercise on some terminal cruise ship. All part of today's entertainment. And I am a terrible, terrible person, that I care about such things.

But I do.

Which makes me hate myself.

Though I hate the blank grey islands of brain damage, that I watch you daily navigate, even more.

I am bad tempered. And in the final weeks of chemotherapy. On the worst day, I lie curled on my bathroom floor, my sister, cool palm on my back, reassuring me, my mother on the other side, telling me I can do this, I can live. But there are days when I am so sorry for myself. When I am limping, joints aching from the paclitaxel that knocks me for six, that gnaws at the bones in my ankles and hips, as I'm struggling to get you to bed, fighting my own nausea and trying to tell myself that all of this is normal, the cancer hasn't metastasised as I fear. Days when I look at you, lying on the hammock in the back garden, enjoying the last of the summer sun, focussed on eating the Fruit Pastille ice lolly in your hand, when I think—

'You're going to outlive me.'

And there is some truth in this.

*

A break in the clouds is Dr A, my elegant oncologist, who has made it her mission to save me. Every two weeks, she adjusts the chemotherapy medication, listens as I tell her I can't feel the end of my toes or fingers, that the soles of my feet feel spongy, that when I walk it feels as if my feet are sinking into the pavement like I'm barefoot on carpet. The good news is my tumour is shrinking. Chemotherapy has not been the violent throwing up and pulling out of hair that films had led me to believe. It is a slow poisoning, a hollowing out, that leaves you crawling up the stairs on the days when your red blood cell count is so low that there's not enough oxygen in your body to make your legs move. When this happens, I go to hospital and lie watching endless crap TV, having a blood transfusion that goes on for hours whilst my mother sweetly walks back and forth from Pret A Manger to bring me tea and chocolate brownies.

One day I am standing in a coffee shop near the BBC, not far from Harley Street, and I hear two TV executives talking idly about writers and my name is mentioned. I turn, surprised, hat pulled over my bald head on a warm October afternoon, ear cocked, listening.

'No, I hear she's on the way out.'

And with that they are gone.

Illness is deeply uncool and uncomfortable. It is only when it hits that you realise the truth of the old adage 'health is wealth'. But what shocks me more is how much I have relied on the brand of family, my family, being part of a family. Healthy father, mother, children, dog. Successful. Happy. On the surface at least. How all these years I have leaned on the anecdotes of family life, amusing moments, domestic comedy, dropped into conversation in whatever work meeting or social soirée I find myself in, delivered with a quiet swagger, which subtly says,

'I'm alright, Jack.'

But we are not alright, we are so far from alright.

We are this broken family.

September: the kids go back to school, and, as happens every second week of the new school year, each house works on a song, to be sung *a cappella* style, and show-cased for one night only at Alexandra Palace. Tash and I have brought Jacob, walking a little ahead of us, pushing his walker, like a baby's buggy without the sling, but with a handy basket for putting shopping in and a flip-down seat when he needs to rest. Occasionally there is the turn of a head, or surprised smile amongst familiar parents as we help him take his seat. Before, Jacob would have been the first to smile, grab the hand of one of Jesse's friends, the first to offer brief yet warm exchanges with a familiar parent. Now he barely holds a gaze, gripping tightly onto his walker, as if nervous that someone passing might spirit it away.

A packed audience fills this wide and high aircraft hangar of a space. On stage, rows and rows of children in uniform file on and off the stage. My mind trips with the litany of concerts and gigs we have been to with our children. But nothing ever compares to these evenings. Jesse and Mabel are up at last, both singing different solos amongst the swaying, clapping rows of kids. It's a Black Eyed Peas, Jessie J mash-up, that is brilliant and fun and wild. We whoop and clap and smile, Jacob a little lost but listening, oddly fragile tonight. Another milestone, another event I never thought he'd make. I remember back to last year and how far he has come. I hold on to these moments, file them under today's wins. And yet at the same time I'm thinking about how we get him out without embarrassing Jesse and Mabel. All of us are still struggling with his shapeshift. No one else knows the effort it has taken to get him there. The choreography required to get a shirt on over his twisted hand, to keep his trousers up when no belt can be found. The simple act of how we manoeuvre him down the grubby stone stairs bringing me out in a cold sweat.

When we are safely back in the car, waiting for the kids to appear through the sea of smiling, proud parents loitering outside, Lisa, a lovely, kind, thoughtful friend and mum, comes hurrying over and taps on the car window. And she smiles at Jacob and he smiles back, recognising her at once, wanting to wind the window down. And the way Jacob leans his arm on the open window, cocked a little, affecting a natural stance, not to give the game away, something he has been taught in his speech and language sessions, breaks my heart. And though she seems unfazed by Jacob's fixed stare and smile, the silence that invariably occurs when Lisa throws him a question and Jacob drops the conversational ball, is painful. The ball that I must pick up, help him bat back.

'Weren't they great?' I prompt Jacob as the kids climb in the back of the car.

'Brilliant.'

There is no easy way to hide Jacob and me, and I feel for our children, trying to reconfigure these strange, bloated people, flailing around doing a kind of doggy-paddle, as we try to keep up the pretence of being the parents who were once indestructible and healthy, when we're clearly dismally failing. And I am so, so proud that when Jesse sees some of his friends, and leaps out to go join them in the pub, he stops, standing with them, and turns back and taps on that window again, and leans in, gripping his dad's hand and, in close fist pump, kisses his dad on the cheek.

'See you later, man.'

In front of everyone. In front of his friends.

And all is not lost.

All is not lost.

We had always wanted more children, more people at the dinner table, conversation that flowed freely. We got a Labradoodle instead.

There are days we both agree that looking after Freestyler, Styler for short, is harder than having a new baby. Styler pisses up the hall walls and chews shoes, but Jacob approaches his relationship with the dog like he approached his relationship with his children. Observing them, watching them, mirroring them, until they succumb. One of the nicest things my mother ever said was how much she liked listening to Jacob talking to the children and hearing the way he listened to them. And this is true. Jacob was an extroverted introvert, most confident in his own home. His joie de vivre and thirst for playful debate and laughter fuelled our mealtimes, often calling across the kitchen to his sidekick, Alexa, to pull up a song that he wanted Mabel or Jesse to listen to.

'Alexa, play Tom Misch . . . Crazy Dream . . .'

And while the music played, lyrics would be debated . . .

'See, he talks about listening to the Pharcyde . . . I said you ought to listen to them,' Jacob might offer. And another bit of music knowledge would be passed from father to son, and Jesse, eating pancakes at the table, would log it.

'Alexa, play the Pharcyde'

And so it would go on.

Now we have blank cards on which I scrawl ideas for conversation, notes about each child, subjects of interest. Football, university choices, music for Jesse. Dance, National Youth Theatre, A-level decision making for Mabel. I nudge these cue cards, designed to spark some light in Jacob's brain, forward at mealtimes. He stares back at me. This is a game Jacob neither knows nor is willing to play. Even the idea of asking a question, even when it's written down and placed in front of him, is now alien, impossible for him to fathom an answer.

So we sit, Jesse and Mabel and I, creating the scaffolding for conversation, hoping Jacob will climb up and join us. And sometimes he does. Sometimes there is a moment that is pure Jacob. A moment of pure sardonic comedy, eyes wide and fixed, locked with surprise, as he passes random comment.

'You look like a Zen master,' pronounced mid-meal, his eyes now on the tuft of facial hair, newly sprouted and groomed, on Jesse's chin.

'Goal,' shouted on his first trip back to Spurs as the crowd roared and Jesse pulled him up onto his feet.

Or the flash of something that makes Jacob stop, as he

shuffles to bed, passing Mabel and barely raising his head. And she will sink a little, resigned, but still try and reach him.

'Love you, Daddy.'

And just when all is lost again, when the silence is painfully, unwillingly accepted,

'To the moon and back, Mabes.'

I mentally add these to the list of 'Firefly Moments', brief sparks of light that remind us Jacob is still there. It's a list that will slowly grow over the months:

> Jacob initiating crossing the room, taking out a glass and pouring himself a glass of water.
> Jacob taking himself upstairs to bed and taking off his shoes and lying down for a sleep on his own without telling anyone.
> Jacob asking, 'How was your day?'
> Jacob saying, 'You look nice.'
> Jacob's insightful response when I tell the children off for bickering.

'But they don't bicker.' And he is right. They don't. I am just tired and am trying to silence them.

There is one supper, when Jesse and Mabel have come up with a game to distil a novel into a tag line of six words. Silly attempts are batted back and forth.

'A love like this, forever doomed.'

'Shark avenges death of surfer lover.'

And then out of his silence—

'He's slowly recovering from his illness,' he offers, quietly proud of his own brilliance.

Another day, Jesse throws out a random line,

'To be or not to be . . .'

Jacob is fixed on his beloved TV. And without looking up from watching *Friends,* the show on constant loop, without missing a beat, he picks up the whole speech where Jesse has left off.

'. . . that is the question:
Whether 'tis nobler in the mind to suffer
The slings and arrows of outrageous fortune,
Or to take arms against a sea of troubles,
And by opposing end them? To die, to sleep—
No more; and by a sleep to say we end
The heart-ache and the thousand natural shocks
That flesh is heir to. 'Tis a consummation
Devoutly to be wish'd. To die, to sleep;
To sleep, perchance to dream . . .'

I often have this feeling that we are standing in our house, and Jacob is lost somewhere in a distant room, on another floor that we can't quite reach. We open the front door, and quickly see the blackened walls, the charred remains of what was our shared life. We creep up the stairs, looking down to see that the kitchen and hall have fallen away. Another floor, another door, wallpaper peeling, paint bubbled on skirting boards.

'Jacob—?' we call out.

'I'm here . . . I'm up here.'

He calls from deep within this burnt-out life. As our bare feet skim charred floorboards, the broken remains and shards of memories, like furniture and scorched trinkets, lie underfoot, caught in the path of the fire. The electrical fault that has caused such devastation, triggered such scorching heat that it has licked every floor and wall. We pick up the remnants of our lives, hold them up to the light, seeing what can be preserved. A quietly painful inventory, a checklist of what was and what is, that I see all of us secretly tick off in our minds: what Jacob can and can't do. What he was and what he is now. We yearn for a question, the drive of a heated debate or even the sound of his laugh. But everything is muted, buried deep under blankets of ash.

Then suddenly you call out again.

It can be a punchline in *Friends* that makes you smile.

An observation over dinner, or we can see you're turning a question over in your mind. We sit and patiently wait for you to retrieve it, to share it. Normally it is nothing more profound than,

'Can I have more chicken?'

At least you say something, want something, reveal some kind of desire, break the endless silence.

Because on the darkest days it is like you are locked in a room, with no awareness that you can . . . that you need to get out. Or worse, I imagine that when we do at last get to your floor, knock on your door and open it, there is nothing left but the gaping hole and splintered beams that once held up our life, and you are gone, vanished, Elvis has left the building. And just when we are ready to give up and grieve—

You call out again.

'The TV is going to go off.'

And one of us will leap up, find the remote, press the right button, mend this rogue fault, a ticking clock in the corner of the screen that tells us the TV is about to go off.

And you will once more withdraw into *Friends*, the episodes watched again and again. *The One with the Princess Leia Fantasy, The One where Ross Says Rachel, the One After Vegas, The One with Joey's New Girlfriend.*

I ask Dr D, the neuropsychiatrist who you will start to see, why you are so devoted to this show. He thinks about it and suggests,

'Well, I suppose it's a nice place to be. People you know. Nothing bad happening.'

And it becomes the resting post for us all, intermittently, in those first few weeks, which are turning into months, now you are home. Whatever time of the day, whatever the mood, one of us will sit, lean up against the arm of a chair, usually en route for work or back from school and just pick up the story, laughing at now familiar jokes. The theme tune is always reverberating through floorboards.

And there are days when I think,

'This is the song that I will murder you to.'

I Google how to poison someone you love.

I consider putting a pillow over your face.

But I have watched the films, where the feet thrash. Enough detective shows to know that they can tell if someone has been suffocated by the spray of blood in the nostril that invariably happens when the brain is deprived of oxygen.

And I don't want to go to prison. Other than the one I am in.

One day, a nice woman, who I don't know well and who knows Jacob even less, tells me,

'It would have been better if he died.'

And I don't say it, but I think,

'This is something I can say, but you can't. Fuck you . . .
Piss off . . .'

There is another list I am writing, called 'The One with
the List'.

The list of things I am angry about.

That I am angry with you about.

Angry that you still don't know me.

Angry you never hug me.

Angry you have no awareness how our lives now work.

Angry you do not care.

Angry you stay silent when the kids need you to talk.

Angry you now sit in the same place on the sofa.

Angry at the dip it leaves in the sofa.

Angry you won't watch any TV other than *Friends*. Not
even *Breaking Bad* which you loved.

Angry you did not die.

This last one is the one I will struggle with most. It's not
unreasonable. It's understandable. But still, I don't like that
I have said it. Feel it.

I know instead I should write a list of things I am grateful
for. I have read the books, or at least skim read, the worthy
books, notable books, good advice, best sellers given by
well-meaning friends. *Bearing the Unbearable*, *The Other
Side of Sadness*, *It's OK That You're Not OK* and Sheryl
Sandberg's *Option B: Facing Adversity, Building Resilience,
and Finding Joy*. And that's not including the tomes for
overcoming cancer. These I use to prop up my laptop when
I watch Netflix late at night.

In 'The One with the List', Ross writes a list of all of Rachel's faults, fat ankles being one.

'God, this show was so unreconstructed,' I think watching it with Jacob, while writing the same list in my mind, imagining a different man, imagining living a different life.

In a second list, Ross writes down all the cons of another person, another life.

Without Rachel.

And it is simple.

One line.

'She's not Rachel.'

I look at Jacob, as we sit side by side, our dinner on our laps.

He has fallen asleep, a yoghurt spoon still in his mouth.

I sit, imagining what it would mean to bail, to live with a different man, in a different life.

And the simple fact would be—

'He's not Jacob.'

I realise these are hardly the words of Kahlil Gibran but in my mind when I consider Option B – to leave, to die, to run, to live another life, it always comes back to this same thought that renders all the rest null and void.

But what really stops me is vocalised by dry-witted Nick, one of Jacob's closest friends, a few months later. Returning from dinner with Jacob, at a little restaurant down the road, I ask him how it went.

'Well, he's not Jacob, but I quite like this guy.'

And I take the yoghurt spoon from your mouth. Turn the TV off. Stand behind you as you shuffle once more to bed.

Despite everything—
Smart boy . . .
Rain Man . . .
This half-dead dad . . .
I quite like this guy.
But—
. . . He's not Jacob.

9

Jacob has a knife through his head.

It is Halloween.

Taking a photo of him standing in our kitchen, beaming, I am proud of how witty I am. The plastic novelty wear I've got him from the Camden party shop we often frequent is a wry nod to all he has been through. The stake through his brain.

'You can be that or a ghost?' I offer, a few minutes before proceedings get underway.

He opts for the knife in the head.

I am the ghost.

It seems apt.

Death narrowly missed.

I thought of dressing as my shrunken tumour but realised, this was a little too sick.

A week before, Dr P had jumped excitedly out of his seat to tell me I have made a complete clinical response. The cancer is nearly gone. Now it's a case of cutting out the debris. And zapping it with radio waves. This, he tells me,

'Is the easy bit.'

We are celebrating something else.

My last chemo.

Jacqui, best buddy, chemo buddy, gives me a balloon.

A giraffe balloon.

I don't entirely know why.

When I sit on the edge of Jacob's bed, I tell Jacob I will be gone a couple of nights for my surgery, and not to worry.

'But I do worry,' he responds furrowing his brow.

Halloween is a precursor to this, the last hurrah.

I wonder if I can still say,

'I have cancer.'

People are nice to you when you say it.

I mourn it a little bit.

One year I dressed up as full gravestone angel. Long silver hair, silver face, grey chiffon shroud. I scared the shit out of little kids, and tripped up, scuffed my knees, the dress too long, the heels too high. Another year, Jacob wore yellow contacts and horns. The devil incarnate, opening the door in Stroud Green. We have very nice neighbours, but some turn their lights off on the last day of October, refusing to answer their doors on this pagan festival. But we, at No. 23, have our pumpkins ready and lit before it's even gone dark. I don't quite know why we both love it so much. It could be to do with the lines of sugar and chocolate we consume as the night unfolds. But I have come to realise it is the one festival without guilt. Neither of us owns Halloween. It is outside of religion – Jewish or Christian. Outside of duty. No family visits or meals necessary.

It is Jacob's favourite festival of the year.

I tell him this.

'No, it's not,' Jacob says.

'Which one is it then?' I ask.

'I don't have one,' he replies.

Still, he throws himself into the spirit of it. I open the

door, and I nod to him to hold out the bowl of sweets, which he dutifully does, with suitable zombie stare.

No one realises he's not even trying.

Children, who once ran around our back garden having water fights and playing in our tree house, now tower as they rap on our door, with facial hair and burly voices,

'Trick or treat?'

Jacob knows many of them, he was often the driver to football matches or the pickup post parties. A neighbour's son, now well into his teens, who hasn't seen Jacob since before his collapse, smiles as he grabs a handful of mini Twixes and Bounties.

'Hi, Jacob.'

Jacob stares blankly back, feigns knowing him.

He doesn't.

He closes the door.

Watches TV.

Eats a lot of sweets.

We play Scrabble. He's not too shoddy.

TRAY

THRIVED

PUKE.

Three of his top scoring words.

He's improving.

I add these to the Firefly Moments list.

It is progress all round this month.

We want to adjust Jacob's medication. We are convinced that the cocktail of seizure and epilepsy drugs, antipsychotics and antidepressants are adding to his lethargy and fatigue. At any given moment Jacob will close his eyes and drop into a deep sleep. In the car, on the sofa, midway through a conversation his lids will droop, and he will slightly snore as we carry on dinner, covering his tracks if we have guests.

Dr Z, one of his brilliant consultant neurologists at the National Hospital, reassures me that the sudden fatigue is a factor in encephalitis recovery. An expert in his field, we talk on the phone, and he offers me a long reading list on the subject. In the early 1920s a pandemic of encephalitis lethargica spread across the world affecting over five million people. In Oliver Sacks' book, *Awakenings*, he vividly describes this condition. It's not the kind that Jacob has, but the similarities in symptoms are, at times, strikingly similar.

They would be conscious and aware – yet not fully awake; they would sit motionless and speechless all day in their chairs, totally lacking energy, impetus, initiative, motive, appetite, affect or desire; they registered what went on about them without active attention, and with profound indifference. They neither conveyed nor felt the feeling of life; they were as insubstantial as ghosts, and as passive as zombies.

Living with Jacob is a lot like living with a ghost. He is part toddler, part elderly dementia-ridden patient, part frustrated teenager, part child, part Jacob. And still mainly silent. There's a lack of drive, of purpose. The soporific pace of his day, which we try and punctuate with ukulele lessons and choir and therapies and trips to the cinema, is always swimming against the tide of fatigue and sleep. Jacob's consultants, a smorgasbord of different disciplines, from epilepsy, to encephalitis, to gastro, neuro and MS, whilst thoughtful and attentive, can only offer Jacob appointments once every six to nine months in an overstretched NHS. They remind us that the first two years are key, that Jacob's recovery will then plateau, that only then will we know how far he has come. But that in the long term, the brain damage may mean some things will never change, some parts may have been lost forever. They crank him up with more medication and send us home. He needs more. We need more. Plus, it's really starting to piss me off, the game we play which I call,

'Am I Abi today?'

The reply is always still,

'No.'

I remember when I was in my teens, my neighbour, an elderly woman called Mrs Peacock, knocked on our door. Rumour had it she was once a prostitute; whether she had been or not, it made for a good story. She wore lipstick smeared on her face and badly applied blue eye shadow (maybe that should have been a giveaway). Someone had broken into her house, and I dutifully peered over the fence and could see, through a window, a man rifling through her desk. My mother called the police, and when they arrived, the man answered the door of her house rather bewildered and, with a resigned frown, revealed he was her son; his mother had clearly done this before. But Jacob is not in his eighties, with dementia. He is forty-seven years old.
We need help.
More help than we are getting.
I'm tired of zombies, ghosts and imposters.
He needs to start remembering me.

*

Our first meeting with Dr D takes place in his fourth floor office in Harley Street. We stop halfway up for Jacob to breathe. Dr D sits on a chair facing a sofa in a large white room filled with several other chairs. He is intriguing and laid back in slim trousers and boots that make him look like one of the Kinks. We've agreed he will talk to us together at first and then I will leave the room and he will talk to Jacob alone. And then Jacob will leave, and he will talk alone with me.

As I sit outside on a dark landing, the murmur of their voices is unintelligible. Still, conversation seems to rumble on, and is mildly soporific, so much so that I jerk awake when the door opens, and Dr D nods for me to return.

Daniel, Jacob's carer, takes him off for a cup of tea, and I settle back in the low sofa, facing Dr D on his highchair. We are at considerably different heights. He admits that he finds Jacob's eloquence with language 'astonishing', considering all that he has been through. I ask if they talked openly about the Capgras and he confirms they did. Dr D has come highly recommended and I am keen for a second opinion. He is clearly intrigued by Jacob and later I read his report.

We spoke about his relationship with Abi. He said he met Abi when he was aged 30. [Abi said when he was 27 or 28.] He initially said he had had no concerns about the relationship. I asked him directly, 'Are you concerned that Abi is no longer Abi?' He said, 'I feel like there was another person.' I asked him when this started. He said he had always felt this since he had been ill. He mentioned that he had been in an induced coma since June 2018 to January 2019 (six months). He felt that she was no longer Abi after the induced coma. Abi left at this point in order for us to discuss this further. He said he had this sense that she was not the old Abi (just as much as the other). I asked him what the mental health team had said about this. He said in the case of encephalitis people are prone to misremember people, and it could be part of the symptoms. He said, 'I don't agree with that.'

I asked him how he felt about his belief that she was different. He said, 'I find it difficult.' I asked whether there were any difficulties in his interactions with Abi now. He said, 'Sometimes.'

I asked whether he could tell me about it. He said, 'It's difficult because she wants me to see her as the real Abi and because I don't it's quite challenging.'

We established that they don't sleep in the same room now and do not have a physical relationship. He said on direct questioning that he would want a physical relationship.

I asked him why he would want to pursue a relationship with Abi as she is now. He said, 'There is a relationship there, but a different person.' I asked what had happened to Abi. He said, 'Abi just went away.' I asked whether he thought this was out of character for her. He said, 'Yes.' I asked why she would do that. He said, 'I don't know.' 'There isn't any reason I can think of.' He said that the 'new Abi is just a different person'. I tried to clarify in what way she was different. He said facially she was different. I pointed out that Abi was now having chemotherapy for breast cancer. I put it to him that she might be the same person, but she has gone through some life changes. He said, 'possibly'. I pointed out that no one else thinks she might be different. We discussed how they had the same conversations, she knows the same things as the old Abi, and she interacts with the children in the same way.

I asked him how he felt about the situation. He said it was difficult and he was sad and had a sense of loss. He was confused but not angry. I asked him why he wasn't angry. He said, 'It's not me.' I asked whether he had made any efforts to find out where Abi was. He said no. I asked him why not. He said, 'I just haven't.' I asked whether the new Abi was a nice person. He said yes. I asked whether she loved him. He said yes. I asked how it made him feel. He said, 'guilty'. I asked why he felt that. He said he felt guilty for 'letting her look after me and love me when I don't see her as the same person'. I asked whether he had discussed the idea with Abi that she wasn't the same person. He said no. I asked why. He said, 'Because it felt like a big can of worms.' I asked whether he had discussed it with anyone apart from professionals. He appeared to contradict his statement that he had not discussed his belief about Abi with her. On questioning, he said he had discussed his beliefs about Abi with 'Just Abi.' I asked what she said about this. He said, 'She finds a way around it.' I asked how she did that. He said, 'I don't know.' I asked him whether he ever felt violent towards Abi. He said no, saying, 'It's not in my way of doing things.'

I like Dr D. I like his honesty. But what really stays with me is his belief not that the Capgras will go but that—
'. . . it will become less useful to him . . .'

I query this, it's intriguing. So far expectations of Jacob ever recognising me again have been grim. But this . . . this makes sense to me. Dr D enlightens me, leaning a little in his chair, legs crossed, head thrown back as if he is mulling on something much deeper than you or I will ever understand, only to discover that the Murray Mint he is eating has got stuck to a back molar.

'In many ways, Jacob's conviction that you are not the real Abi Morgan is a little like a religious conversion. No amount of reasoning will change the absolute belief he holds.'

I probe beyond this road-to-Damascus revelation, for anything else.

'I did ask him if he found this Abi attractive,' he offers.

'And?'

'ish . . .' he replied.

Jewish, wellish, cancerish . . . I hunger for certainties. To sit squarely in a religion, a diagnosis, a marriage, a third act. Yet here we are, hovering. A few months earlier, when the weather is still hot and sticky, and I am bracing myself for chemo, I scroll through my iPhone, pounding the streets, blindly doing circles, as is sometimes Google Maps' evil way. At last, I find my destination, a narrow slither of a house, nestling between large red-brick Victorian terraces, in upper Hampstead. Laura answers the door, a warm, eager, bright-eyed former nanny, now a sound and energy therapist who has come highly recommended by a friend.

'I really think she is something special, she's worked

with a number of cancer patients and had extraordinary results.'

And she is something special. Very special and lovely. But first she talks. A lot. Then listens as I talk. A . . . lot . . . picking up on the details of the now well-hashed narrative of Jacob's collapse and fight to survive, upended by my stage 3 cancer diagnosis. But I am to be reassured. There is a grey-haired man . . . we have them . . . these ghostlike figures . . . from a past . . . from a future . . . spirit guides. This one is quite possibly my father, looking over me . . . I am to know he is around. Also, eagles . . . and bees . . . Bees are going to be important . . . They are symbols of diligence, activity, work, good order, empowerment . . . I am to look out for bees . . . And feathers . . . white feathers, sent by the angels to reassure us, to be now forever caught and pocketed, along with the balled-up tissues and chocolate wrappers.

I drink it up. Grateful*ish*, sceptical*ish*, worried*ish* . . .

This is a woman who has had her own battles, a chronic childhood illness, who throws a rope ladder out to me, to which I cling. Slowly the *ish* dissolves like fret into sand until our conversation melds into a wash of words that bind me, soothe me and I find myself lying on a massage table while she circles me, bathing me in sound radiating from tuning forks that she holds in her hands and lightly taps.

I think I fall in love with her a bit.

'Bonkers . . . this is bloody bonkers . . . What are you doing?' I hear Jacob quietly whispering in my ear which I determinedly ignore.

'Ssh . . . Fuck off . . .' I reply.

210

'Seriously?' his brows furrowed with a smile.

This is the madness that accompanies exile.

Where Jacob has left me, I find him in my mind.

'Run . . . This is desperate,' he mocks.

'So, let me be desperate.'

Let me stay swimming through this sea of vibrations.

Let me lie.

One birthday, Jacob gave me a card, marked out with a word search. My present to be found. As I ringed, and re-ringed, letter after letter, I told myself this is it, the great proposal.

It wasn't.

As I continued to circle letters and then words, there was a proposal in there. Just not the romantic kind.

TRAPEZE

JUGGLING

TIGHTROPE WALKING

'A fucking circus skills course?' I hurl, when any other hope had been scored out.

And the look, quizzical, as it dawned on him that this long-thought-out birthday gift was not the much-wanted welcome surprise.

'But you said you wanted something different . . . Outside of your comfort zone,' he offers.

'I spend my life juggling plates, you doofus,' I reply.

A circus skills course, begrudgingly accepted through gritted teeth and tense smile and further proof of our differences to be added to the lists of our opposing likes and dislikes that we struggle to reconcile.

<u>My observations on him.</u>
Random acts of madness. See circus skills course.
Refusal to appreciate the meditative quality of *Keeping Up with the Kardashians* and the social anthropological value of sidebar of shame. Aka *Daily Mail* online.
Dislike of anchovies. Shows lack of sophistication.
Thumb sucker. TBD. Not attractive in a father or grown-up man.
<u>His observations on me.</u>
Random acts of kindness, that usually involve long car journeys to distraught friends and parking fines.
Dumbing down. See *Kardashians* and *Mail* online.
Matcha. Who doesn't like matcha – tea or otherwise?
Sense of humour failure. TBD. Not attractive in a grown-up woman. Not attractive full stop!!!
But I wouldn't change the memory that circus course gave me.

The mental snapshot of Jacob knelt outside a rundown gymnasium in some dodgy arse end corner of East London, on a wet pavement, with Jesse and Mabel, aged five and three, their noses pressed to the glass of a steamy window looking in at me standing atop a five-tier pyramid of bored housewives and lonely accountants. The pure unadulterated beaming smiles of their joy and pride.

I will push myself out of any emergency exit. Hurl myself down any inflated slide. Take myself out of any comfort zone into some bonkers, twinging and twanging sound bath, if, for just a few minutes, I can be back in a life that was as simple and as beautiful as two little children, giggling and marvelling at their mother, teetering and spilling out of ridiculous unflattering neon Lycra, basking in their pride.

Because I want peace.

I want reassurances.

And I will even take my dead dad spirit guide.

Yeah, I'm out of my comfort zone.

You were my comfort zone.

So what the hell do I do now?

There is a scene in the film *Truly Madly Deeply* written and directed by Anthony Minghella that I keep coming back to. It was the early 1990s and I was newly arrived in London. I watched it on a rainy afternoon in an empty screen at the Odeon, Leicester Square, with no money and no more excuses as to why I did not write, even though I knew it might well be the only way I would get out of waitressing for the rest of my life. Juliet Stevenson plays Nina, an interpreter working at a chaotic language school, so tormented by grief following the sudden death of her cellist boyfriend Jamie that she conjures him back in the form of a ghost. After the joy of the reunion, Nina and Jamie resume their love affair. But as the days turn into weeks, Nina comes to see that Jamie, trapped in this nocturnal existence, and now with several of his ghost friends also moved in, no longer fits into her life. Nor she into his.

A meditation on grief, Nina navigates the language of loss as the exquisite notes of Bach's Cello Sonata No. 3 drift through the house, haunting her. I find myself watching it again, late one night. In one of the final scenes Nina comes to see that they, quite literally now, live in two different places, both of them caught between the living and the dead. She returns from the birth of a friend's baby to find that Jamie and his ghost friends have rolled back the carpet and are considering sanding the floorboards. This is the final straw. Nina throws the friends out. She and Jamie are finally alone, Jamie perched on the rolled carpet, Nina on the stripped wooden floorboards, finally admitting that they are at sea.

'Was it like this before?' Nina asks.

'What?' replies Jamie.

'Before? Were we like this?'

Jamie reassures her. She's tired. She's been up all night. Her friend has just had a baby.

Yet Nina persists.

'You see I . . . I held that baby . . . it's so . . . It's life . . . It's a life I want . . . And all my taste . . . all my things . . . after you died, I found stuff in my trunk that I'd put there because you disapproved . . . or laughed at . . . Books . . . photographs and things . . . I couldn't . . . I didn't know how to mend a fuse or find a plumber or bleed a radiator . . . But now . . . I can and . . . I so much longed for you . . . I longed for you . . .'

Jamie suspects what she is trying to say and as a way to demonstrate his understanding he asks her to translate a poem for him.

The Dead Woman by Pablo Neruda.

No, forgive me.
If you no longer live,
if you, beloved, my love,

if you
have died,
all the leaves will fall on my breast,
it will rain on my soul night and day,
my feet will want to walk to where you are sleeping,
but
I shall stay alive

I look around our living room. There is a new chair, a midnight purchase in the early months when you were febrile and restless in hospital and I was equally febrile and restless at home. Photographs of Jacob and the children rearranged on top of a shelf. The addition of four new cushions – orange Marimekko poppies which you would hate. Black and grey Tom Dixon which you may have hated slightly less. In the hallway I have moved the white table. I've given away the green sofa we only bought a couple of years ago, but which no longer fits in our living room, now we have a day bed for carer or guest.

Upstairs, I have rearranged our bedroom, bought another chair, pink, which I think you might like. A new salt cellar now stands on our kitchen island. A yellow jug, packed away, and then refound, which you always thought was too tall for our shelves. There has been a slow recolonisation of the space, the quiet shift of object or painting just a couple of inches to the right. And as I have moved things, with the furious industry which you used to observe, and at times distract me away from in favour of some other weekend fun, I thought it was because I was setting the stage for your return. In truth, I have been marking out the blueprint for this new lopsided life. With you here, but not here. Me standing to the left, you to the right, wondering as I guide you past a doorway or upstairs if you will notice these minor adjustments, these quiet rebellions, that have been purchased and reordered through the prism of what I like.

Because I too packed away part of myself when I met you.

Doesn't everyone within a long relationship?

Within the confines of marriage?

Adjust?

Conform?

Compromise?

But you never do notice. Not even when the green sofa is moved out. Not even when, after several weeks of walking up to bed, I point at a photograph taken the Christmas when you were sleeping, locked in a coma. It's of my entire family seated like the Last Supper on our orange bench, a garland of paper lanterns strung overhead. You peer at it and then nod resigned, despatched to another time, another history, another photograph from a different life. One you walk past, graze through, but which you neither own nor feel territorial over. No longer recognising that the woman in the photographs is me, that you are you. Photos in cities and countries we have visited, memories of birthdays and holidays and high days which, when I ask, you say you remember, can even accurately add details, but which you remember as if lived by another person. And I am reminded that alongside the ghost of you, the ghost of us, there is the ghost of our past life.

Every night I help you to bed, take off your trousers, your socks, your shoes, tuck you in, check the plastic bottles that you pee in are by your bed. I have taken to kissing you on the forehead or cheek, not daring to hover close to your lips, reserved for the other Abi Morgan, the other life.

'Good night, Mr Magoo,' I say.

'Good night,' you reply.

And I wish you'd call me Abi. I wish it so much you see me cry. And you look at me with such confusion, such concern, as I sob, perched on the end of your bed, that you tear up too.

'Have you hurt yourself?' you say.

'Yes,' I nod. 'Yes.'

Tomorrow, I am going to hospital to have my left breast removed and I am crying not because I am scared, but because you will never see me as I was. A vital bit of evidence to prove I am the real Abi Morgan will be gone. And I, like this world we live in now, will be unsymmetrical, lopsided, depleted, one breast down, my body, like your brain, disfigured.

'I'm going to hospital tomorrow, Jacob,' I say.

He nods, thinking on this, staring up at the ceiling.

'I'm going to have a mastectomy, Jake.'

'Oh dear.' He looks at me, worried again.

It crosses my mind that he might want to see it, my left breast, wave it off. It's a thought I share. And his look, his look is one of utter horror.

'No thank you,' he grimaces. 'I don't think she'd like it.'

'Who, Jacob? Who won't like it?'

I push a little more, already knowing what comes next.

'Abi Morgan,' he sighs.

I saw a ghost once. When Jesse was no more than two. And I was now working on an adaptation for screen of a brilliant and beautiful memoir, *If the Spirit Moves You*, by Justine Picardie, sister of Ruth Picardie, the author discussed when I first met Jacob at that dinner party. Justine's memoir captures the story of how she tried to connect with her sister Ruth, following her death. So ghosts were on my mind. Jacob and I were sleeping in the room next door to Jesse, when I woke, thirsty. I padded to the bathroom in search of water. As I turned, at the end of the long landing I saw a curly-haired boy, small, no more than four or five. He was dark, caught in the shadows, but peering out of the study doorway. I called out.

'Jesse?'

Nothing, but for the strange sound of friction, the kind of friction that is made when you rub dry palms together.

I put my head around Jesse's door and see his small bumpy form, caught in the tangle of duvet and zebra, the stuffed animal he will carry with him for most of his childhood. I look back along the dark landing towards the open doorway. My heart is thumping now, because as I walk slowly towards it, the friction is gathering in pace and sound. Until, shaking now, I reach out a hand and flick the light switch on. And at once, all drops to silence. The room is at once starker and more familiar, a back bedroom I use for writing. No figures hidden by curtains, no furniture offering a place to hide. I flick the light back off again and, as I walk back along the corridor, I tell myself I must be hallucinating.

As I turn, I see the little boy again, once more peering around, looking at me, still dark and caught in the shadows, but so clear now that I can see the thick curls of his hair, and the edging of his pyjamas, reminding me of some

1970s football shirt. When I look again the boy is gone. I hurried back into bed, stuck my cold feet against Jacob's calves, rolled over, lay quietly. And in the morning, I tell Jacob the story, which he enjoys but which he puts down to too many sleepless nights.

Months later, I will talk to an elderly neighbour and she will tell me that the family who once lived in our house fostered a number of children and that one of those children died in the house. A little boy, no more than four or five.

I do not believe in ghosts.

I do not believe in heaven or the afterlife.

Later, when we send the film script to an eminent Taiwanese director, he will respond positively but will in the end decline, by email, with words to the effect, that there is no tension in a story that is built around a character whose whole experience is dependent on finding out if there is an afterlife. As a Buddhist, he goes on to say, he lives with ghosts by his side, their world, as it does, overlapping with ours.

It occurs to me that this is how I move through our house now. Peering around doorways, spooking Jacob, waiting for him to walk back along the landing, turn on the light. To see that she is gone, the ghost of Abi Morgan is gone, and that this person, this person is now his . . . partner . . . wife. Because as much as we are all trying to bring Jacob back, time is pulling us forward. Or rather the very real sense I now have of my mortality and the temporary nature of life means I can't go back.

I don't want to go back.

It's life I want.

Life.

Tomorrow Dr P is going to remove the last of my cancer. I am practical, unemotional about this, but still. Something that was attached to me, that was a given, that I have largely ignored, something will be irrevocably changed, taken, cut out, off, removed. But if it means I will survive? Then it is alright. As I leave the house the next morning with my sister, I want to run back to Jacob. I want to tell him to wake up. I want him to tell me, there is no such thing as ghosts. There is only you and me and this life. But as I pass his bedroom doorway, I can hear him talking, sleeping and talking, caught in his own kind of afterlife—

'Yeah, babe . . . Well, give it to me and I'll take it . . .'

I listen, my ear close to his door.

Babe . . . Only ever used now when he is sleeping.

'No . . . No . . . You did it last time.'

Yes, we live with the ghosts by our side, their world, as it does, overlapping with ours.

And I am on my own.

I am doing this on my own.

Only as I turn to leave, I hesitate on seeing—

A bee sitting on my front doorstep.

Bees are going to be important . . .

Symbols of diligence, activity, work, good order, empowerment—

I side-step it and climb into the Uber.

7 a.m. and all is still dark outside.

10

I need a drink.

I stopped drinking in early 2016 for a while. Two years before Jacob's collapse. Not because I was an addict. Or even because I was concerned I had a real problem. I was just bored of being embarrassed. Once every couple of years, there would be a spectacular drunken fail, which people forgave. I couldn't forgive it anymore. After a difficult day at work, a delicate political situation navigated, I went out for a glass of wine. Several hours and glasses later, a detour to a karaoke bar and a fatal late-night last-minute espresso martini, I found myself passed out, my head wedged between two parked cars in a street half a mile from my home at 2 a.m. I had stumbled out of the taxi, somewhere just past the Emirates Stadium, concerned I was going to vomit. I didn't and congratulated myself in the morning that I had made my way home, wallet and phone and body still in one piece. But the graze on my cheek and shadow of a black eye was not a good look for a woman a few years shy of fifty.

Jacob took me out to a local Japanese restaurant for a workday lunch, and I sobbed into my miso. I gave up that day and, bar the odd mournful wave of nostalgia for a bottle of Jacob's Creek that can still knock me for six in my local Londis, sobriety has been what it says on the tin. Though I am grateful for every fun night and spectacular story alcohol gave me, the state of being sober, or quality of being staid or solemn, is not without its gifts. And though I tell myself I will drink again, which I do, in a few months' time, I don't think I will ever gaily trip into the drunken nights of hedonism of the past. Call it growing up, but as my children become teenagers two thoughts suddenly become clear. 1) Being sober means I am always on hand to pick them up if and when they get drunk, and can be rightfully magnanimous as I steer them, now dressed in someone else's clothes, home. 2) I can still talk shit at parties, the difference is now I remember it.

Still, I miss people, fun.

We need fun.

'We're having a party, Jake.'

It's November again.

'What do you think?'

You have just poured yourself a large bowl of Crunchy Nut cornflakes, which you do every morning now. Always the same weekday breakfast, piled high and then levelled with the top of your right hand. One of the many repetitive traits, some might say rituals, you have developed, which I quietly note, adding them to my list. In a few minutes you will pour milk, from the two-litre plastic bottle you have also brought to the island in the middle of our kitchen. You have been working on this simple breakfast routine, bowl, spoon, Crunchy Nut, milk, with Helen, your brilliant down-to-earth and ever-calm OT. Along with the Chinese stir fry which I am yet to sample but which you make at lunchtime with Helen supervising. A cognitive jigsaw puzzle that can be painful to watch as you weigh up noodles, saucepan, hot water.

My question, however, has broken your flow.

You look at me, then back at the two-litre plastic bottle of milk.

'Sorry,' I say apologetically.

You nod, begrudgingly accept my apology, and resume pouring milk. A delicate bit of cereal choreography as the bowl is so high, flakes can topple. Which you must then slowly retrieve, put back in the bowl, replace the milk in the fridge, then carry the bowl over to the table, where finally you sit and begin eating.

'It's to celebrate you. And to thank everyone. Who visited and helped us, Jacob?'

I've done it again.

You look up, mid-mouthful, spoon poised, eyes narrowing like Paddington Bear, considering the odds of me shutting up and your getting through the whole bowl in the silence you prefer.

'There'll be cake.'

You pause, the spoon hovering dangerously close to your mouth.

'What kind of cake?'

As we know, I do this.

Have random parties.

Rainbow cakes in the park, even when the guest of honour is otherwise indisposed.

Birthdays, Christmas gatherings, BBQs, dinners. One year we parked an ice-cream van in our drive. No reason, just the sheer joy of giving out ice creams to guests and passers-by. Jacob plays along, orders beer, buys meat, refills gas canisters, mulls wine, whilst never entirely convinced he is going to enjoy any of it. But he always does. And at the end of the night, when I have spent most of it wiping humus off my face, topping up glasses and avoiding conversation, Jacob will be filled with stories of the chats and laughs with friends and family that I have missed, so busy have I been emptying beer bottles into bin bags and finding coats as guests leave.

Only this party is different.

Because the truth is, this party isn't for him. It's for me. Jacob is my beard. It's all part of the constant 'I'm alright, Jack, what's it like to have everything, we've survived this and aren't I fan-fucking-tastic, madame OBE Morgan, it's not enough to survive, life is to be lived!' shit.

I'm fooling no one.

Still, cakes are ordered, scones are baked, fizz is iced. We even have a pianist. A very sweet young man my mother has just finished working with. He tinkles on the ivories in our living room whilst we chat and drink and eat cake. And I think 'I've missed this.' This feeling of being part of something, friendly with friends, rather than friendless. Alone with silence and Crunchy Nut cornflakes. And of course, Rachel and Ross and Chandler, Phoebe, Monica and Joey. I want to feel like myself again. Us, for us to feel like ourselves again. I want Jesse and Mabel to see that our life does go on.

'It's not enough to survive, you've got to live . . .'
Perhaps not so crazy or crap after all.

Also, Jacob has agreed to write a speech. With the aid

of Amina, who grips the task with the fervour of Hildy Johnson in *His Girl Friday*. I can hear the murmur of her voice as she reads back to him what she types and also, I suspect, writes for him.

On the day, Jacob sleeps, as we fluff and plump and generally put the house in order, bringing it back to life with the flurry and excitement of a first night, all hands on deck. My family, Jacob's family and a select gathering of sixty or more friends. I put on a shirt, which in combination with my bald head, makes me look like the Dalai Lama. I take the shirt off and put another one on, this time without looking at myself in the mirror. I, like Jacob, now catch my reflection in whatever glass surface I am passing, with the same mixture of discomfort and surprise, not entirely convinced that the way I look is a true representation of what is going on inside.

But it is, I look as I feel.

Bumpy.

Bald.

Exposed.

Depleted.

Yet not without the hope of regrowth, a few grey tufts of hair starting to sprout and speckle the white skin of my head. And Jacob is improving, I pass him in the hallway, a vase of flowers in hand. He, just down from getting dressed and freshened up for the arrival of guests that is only minutes away.

'You look nice,' he says.

Amina smiles encouragingly at me, which is what happens when Jacob does or says something pleasant now. As if saying 'Look . . . It's happening . . . He's coming back.'

'So do you, Mr K,' I reply.
He nods, catching Amina's eye, a mutual internal fist pump, job done. The insecurities creep in, and my internal voice whispers,
'You old ham.'
I have stopped trusting him.
I used to trust no one more.
I change my shirt for the third time.

Clothes have always been a moot point for me. There were evenings when I would be sunk in a heap of cast-aside outfits, flushed and infuriated because nothing looked right, already late for dinner or a theatre trip, and a myriad of other nights I ruined with this dress choosing fiasco. In these moments, Jacob would perch himself on a chair and wait for me to cool down, watching me rage.

'Use your words . . . you're good at that,' he'd say with a smile.

And then calmly we would go through my wardrobe and usually we would find something that, I would concede, would do, and he would reassure me that I looked nice, often standing behind me with a weary smile.

'Ready, misery?' he'd say, car keys in hand.

Now I struggle to find things that Jacob can wear. Shoes that will fit over swollen feet, T-shirts that will cover his widening belly, sweaters that will pull over his twisted hand. But his old clothes, he will never wear these clothes again. Sometimes, when I come home and the day has been particularly bad, I stand in the dark, not putting on the light, and lean into them, letting them take my full bodyweight until they are crushed against the back of the closet and my nose is almost flat to the wall.

That, that scene will be cut from the movie.

Too much of a cliché . . .

Think better. Do better.

You can do better.

So, as the weeks move on, Jesse, Mabel and I quietly colonise them. A fleece jacket now worn by Jesse as he heads out to the pub with friends. A sweatshirt, now Mabel's, distressed on the arms so that it looks like the dog and moths have fought over it, but which I discover was eye-wateringly expensive and is meant to be like that. Green khakis, still with the tag on, which I try on, just so I can see if they fit me. They do. I walk past and think I see Jacob notice, but can't quite place why. He was a cool dresser. Loved clothes. Now I am happy if he looks clean and looked after, with some semblance of his former style. And he does. That is the weird thing, throughout all of this, he is familiar, even when he is not.

As guests arrive, I relax. To be frank, I think few of them expected to see Jacob again. The jury is still out on me. Because in part we are also celebrating the end of chemotherapy, and the nearing of the end of my treatment. Soon, the house is filled with laughter and conversation, music and a warmth which reminds me why we do this. A good party is an energy giver, a reset. And our family and friends, from every walk of our lives, arrive ready to have fun, to commit to this party in the way we do to a wedding, wishing the couple well, not entirely sure if they will survive it. But it is brilliant, to feel the house full, to feel the house sing.

All the while, Jacob sits on the orange bench in the kitchen, like some small-time mafia head or minor president. The family flank him, as bodyguards do, bending down to whisper a name like they are discreetly slipping money into his palm, as another 'associate' greets him or seeks counsel. The associates, aka our friends, sit close, smile and squeeze, the delight seemingly mutual. Yet I know there are some people here who Jacob is struggling to locate.

'Who's that?' Jacob whispers quietly to me after they have moved on to another conversation or slice of cake.

'*Oslo*. Last year. Played opposite you. Nice man,' I offer in hushed reply, distracted by another arriving guest. And Jacob either nods, or looks wistfully off into the middle distance, as if deciding whether they make the cut or should go 'swim with the fishes'. Yet in their presence he is the consummate performer, smiling sweetly, letting them grip his hand, nodding and raising his eyebrows a little, mirroring their movement, as he has been taught to do.

His voice definitely has more inflection now. And there is more expression. He cocks his head a little to the right, if you have said something witty or if he wants to show you his surprise, something I know his speech and language therapist has been working on. But still, in a later exam-ination with an ENT specialist, they will tell us that Jacob now has the voice box of a seventy-five-year old, there's been so much damage, even to his vocal chords. Every night, as I walk behind him watching him shuffling up the stairs to bed, I am shaken to my core at the lack of spring in his step. And it is then that I see Jacob, the Jacob I knew, the one always bounding up the stairs ahead of me, the one who once said to me his great fear was,

'That I won't keep up with you.'

That Jacob, that Jacob, stops and looks back at me, helping his shuffling doppelganger to bed, incredulous. That Jacob calmly whispers in my ear,

'Run.'

The ting of a knife against a glass punctures conversation. Guests drawn to attention, now all huddled in our kitchen. I worry about the pianist still tinkling away to an audience of one, in our living room. I feel bad he may feel unappreciated and lonely. Someone clearly tells him, and the room falls quiet.

I think I speak.

I probably speak. Thank people, thank our families, thank our children. Today I am thankful, my inner narcissist jumping up and down on her highchair and screaming—

'Look, we have friends. We are popular. People still like us.'

But who can turn down an invite from the brain damaged and cancer ridden?

I nod to Jacob. It is his turn. He looks to me blankly, so I sit down next to him on the bench and slide his speech in front of him. It is sweet. And thankful. Of his family. His children. Of me. But it is written in a language that I know is not Jacob's. We clap. And hug. Whoop and cheer. The boy's done good. And he remembered, though prompted, to thank me. Later I realise, just under the bench where we are sitting, is the Emmy, still in its box, that I've never taken out.

'Did I thank him today?' I wonder again.

Shit . . . Shit . . .

I place my hand on his knee, and can feel him shaking, his nerves catching me by surprise. In life, Jacob and I played a constant game of hide and seek, leapfrogging behind one another. Using one another as life's shield. First nights, parents' evenings, family dinners, whoever was up that day led, did the talking, while the other hid behind. Today, when I feel Jacob's knee trembling against mine, I'm relieved he's nervous.

That he feels something.

Last night I tried to have a proper conversation with him. A problem with work or life or family, I can't even remember what it was. The meal is over, the table is cleared, the kids already heading to the pub or out with friends. Whilst he sits alone at the table, staring at me as I fill the dishwasher, his brow furrows, perturbed as I seek his opinion.

'What do you think, Jacob?'

It's a director, a difficult director, whose expectations I can't meet.

'Give him time. Don't speak' I say to myself, as I have been told by the therapists to do with Jacob.

'Let him feel the uncomfortable silence.'

I wait a little more, letting the question hang, knowing these are the prompts we have to set up now.

'Jacob?'

He stares back at me, vacant.

Blank.

Nothing.

Another island of damage reached.

Reasoning crashed against rocks.

I nod resigned, turning away from him, tears stinging, shoving gravy-stained forks into the machine, shoulders ready to buckle. Suddenly he gets up, walks towards me, and for a moment I am hopeful until he takes a swing to the left, shuffling towards the sofa in the other room.

'Where are you going?' I call after him.

Silence.

'Jacob?'

'To finish *Spiderman*.'

There are wins.

Gifts to Jacob's strangeness.

A brilliance to Jacob's ability to sing without prompting, loud and often tuneless, whenever a piece of music comes on the car radio or at the end credits of a film. The wonderful Rhia comes into our lives to get him playing ukulele again when he starts to flex his fingers a little more. There's a strange conflicted heart-breaking joy to opening the front door at the end of the day and hearing Jacob's rendition of *The House of the Rising Sun*. His left hand twisted and immobile, Rhia strumming along on Zoom on his iPad, the dog perched on the sofa howling. Or on a Saturday night, at the end of the movie, watching him singing along to *Hey Jude* as the credits roll, realising that this is the bit he enjoys most. Head fixed, yawning he is so tired, yet determinedly reading every name from cameraman to grip, until we are down to the final credits, pillow perched on his belly covered with a tea towel, and the residue of ice cream, that he's just had for tea, in his beard.

Another day, Mabel is rehearsing *Guys and Dolls* for the school musical in which she'll be playing Miss Adelaide. Jacob is already on the second bar of *Take Back Your Mink* before we've even scrolled it up on Alexa, banging it out, heartfelt and flat, with us looking on. Oddly, we take him to *Hamilton*, and he snores through every brilliant song. But on hearing it on Alexa a few weeks later, he knows the words and sings it loud and heartily.

One evening, Christmas Eve, I search for candles, realising it is also the first night of Hanukkah, particularly late this year. Kippah, the small silk hats worn for Jewish festivals, are found, and I film Jacob as he sits perched on a high stool next to Mabel as she lights the candles and he sings the blessing, word perfect, lilting but so out of tune that I can see Jesse in the corner of the frame, turning, trying to stifle nervous laughter, not wanting to put his dad off his game.

Baruch atah Adonai Eloheinu Melech ha-olam, shehecheyanu v-ki'y'manu v-higianu la-z'man ha-zeh.

We are protective of Jacob, as he hovers between man and child. And in many ways, he is the lucky one, unaware of what our privilege affords, with his therapists and ukulele teachers and Alexa on hand to pitch in and find the song. I don't know how anyone does this without support. I know how lucky we are – even now. I am not blind to other tragedies in the world. At night, amidst the Google searches and medical detective work I continue to pursue, I read and watch the news, take in the terrible injustices happening globally, politically, racially, ethically. The condescending chorus that seems to berate those who are 'woke'. As if there is a danger in waking up, staying awake, seeing the world more clearly, wanting to change it. It crosses my mind I have been sleep-walking long before Jacob's collapse. In my myopic world I question what I could have done differently. What *we* could have done differently.

'Question everything. Learn something. Answer nothing.' I read this on a peeling fridge magnet, embellished with a pink kitten, paw thoughtfully scratching its head, stuck to the wall behind the desk of my doctor's receptionist. I later learn it's a quote from Euripides.

Early December and the angry stitches that hold together the skin where my left breast once was, are starting to dissolve. But still my chest looks butchered. The thick black arrow, drawn on my chest by Mr P with a fat magic marker, is still visible just below my collar bone, pointing to where my cancerous breast once was, to ensure they got the right one. I don't try and scrub it but let it fade. The skin is stretched and buckled in a strange way, pulled so tight across my ribs that at night my heart is almost visible beneath translucent scar tissue. I hear it thumping, blood pumping in my head. I don't hate it. In some ways, it feels right. I am literally missing something. And I am proud of the scar. It is fitting. It is a legacy. It will come with me to the grave. I do not reconstruct, squeamish of implants, preferring to be able to see where danger lurks, not wanting it hidden if the cancer returns.

'Why you?' people say.

That question again.

'Why not?'

Shit happens.

A constellation of incidents and misfortunes, genetics and lifestyle aligned.

And we got unlucky.

Jacob got unlucky.

'I'm not angry,' I tell myself.

But this didn't *just* happen.

Jacob didn't *just* get unlucky.

Dr C, Jacob's MS consultant, has a gift for us. We have not seen him for months. He has agreed to meet Josh and me on a cold wintery afternoon, at the porter's lodge of the National Hospital. A wood-panelled reception room to the left of the small chapel where Jacob would go to sing with his group, just yards away from MITU. Jenae, the beautiful young girl two beds from Jacob, is still in intensive care and I meet Collette her mother, swapping stories like long-distance runners, comparing speeds and times.

It is already dark outside. Dr C is waiting for us, pacing a little. He is a gentle man, thoughtful, keen to know Jacob's progress, hopeful. After preliminary small talk, he slides Jacob's notes across the table. Amongst them is a copy of a report that Dr M, the nice Irish consultant there in the early days at MITU, informed me was being written in August. Jacob's case has been published in a medical journal, written by Dr C and his team, along with an acknowledgement of the probability of the link between the MS drug and Jacob's collapse.

We report a case of anti-NMDA receptor encephalitis, occurring fourteen weeks after the mandated discontinu-

ation of treatment with the drug with which he had been successfully treated for four years.

Josh and I read on.

Secondary CNS autoimmune complications of the drug treatment were first reported to the European Medicines Agency (EMA) in February 2018, following which the drug was voluntarily withdrawn in March 2018. Although the initial EMA report in March 2018 suggested 12 potential cases of encephalitis or encephalopathy, a revised report in May 2018 identified 9 cases (5 German, 2 American, 1 Swiss and 1 Australian) where the causality of the drug could not be ruled out. In one patient NMDA receptor antibody was identified. All cases share similar clinical pictures of devastating or fatal outcome (2 cases), lack of responses to first line (corticosteroid, plasma exchange, intravenous immunoglobulin) and second line (rituximab) treatments, and unusual findings on brain biopsy.

21 people with devastating or fatal outcomes.

Jacob makes it 22.

I can't sleep that night. In my head I angrily graffiti a list of losses. A tally of all Jacob can no longer do. It stretches on.

Can't act.

Can't drive.

Can't cut his own food.

Can't walk for long distances.

Can't have sex.

Can't use a computer.

Can't talk to his children.

Can't talk to anyone without the other person building the conversational climbing frame.

Can't get himself out of bed.

Can't dress.

Can't tie his own shoes.

Can't stay awake through *Hamilton*. *Hamilton*? Please . . .

Can't do much.

Can't be the dad, husband, son, brother, uncle, friend he was.

Can't remember me.

Weirdly, it's the 'can't act can't drive' that gets me the most.

Jesse passes his driving test just before Christmas, and I sell the soft-top Mini that Jacob gave me. I now worry that the open top and daily drives to Jacob in hospital got me nicely burnished in rain and shine but did nothing for my cancer or air pollution. I buy Jesse a cleaner car, and there is a joy in seeing him whizzing his dad up and down the hill our house perches on, knowing for Jacob this is the next best thing to being behind the wheel himself. Still, I used to love the long drives, stroking the back of his neck as we listened to the radio coming back from whatever day trip or Soho shopping venture we had gone on. The 'can't act' bit is harder to resolve.

Jacob was just coming into his own in the months before

his collapse. He had weathered years of watching my plays, sitting in the audience as my career flourished. It was nice as the world turned and he was the one on the stage. When we first met, and the work was sparse, we came up with another list of other work he could do. There was a mad morning when we even discussed him going into medicine at forty-three, but it always came back to the same thing. Acting was the only thing he thought he could do. Which wasn't true. But that's the way for actors. The tendrils cling deep.

It is September 2011. I am at the Venice Film Festival. *Shame*, a film I have co-written, is premiering. A giddy few days, eating delicious pasta and taking in the Biennale, but all the time, Jacob is ill in hospital. He reassures me that it is nothing serious. I film the cast sending a Get Well message to Jacob. Three weeks later it is confirmed that it is his first serious MS relapse. It is filed away, pushed to the back of the drawer, but over the years his condition grazes our life with increasing regularity. Even so, Jacob didn't dwell on it and when the relapses happened, they were managed and less difficult than the first. If anything, the diagnosis made him run faster, dig deeper, work harder to enjoy life. The opportunity to join the last phase of a drugs trial seemed hopeful. And certainly, for the first couple of years, he did well. Well enough for the drugs trial to be extended. Once a month he went for his injection to Queen Square. We rarely talked about it.

In the January before his seizure, the children and I proudly watch Jacob playing Yossi Beilin in *Oslo*, a pithy, beautifully composed play by J. T. Rogers about the Oslo Peace Accords between Israel and the PLO, first at the National Theatre and later at the Harold Pinter Theatre in the West End. The dressing rooms are compact and zigzag off a narrow corridor. Jacob struggled to hide his fatigue from the other actors. Jacob was always fearful this would somehow undermine a director's or fellow actor's confidence in him. But late at night, the throbbing headaches and cramps would floor him. I would once more hurl paracetamol through the bedroom door.

Hence the whole 'You are a terrible nurse' thing.

It was a secret kept from most people.

To know that it was made worse by the drug that was meant to help him, makes me sadder than anything.

'Well, even Nurofen has a black box warning. They have to test on someone,' a helpful voice offers one day.

'Yeah, and Jacob's not a fucking lab rat.'

And I am angry.

Angrier than I want to admit.

Jesse and Mabel are sixteen and eighteen within ten days of one another. It's late January, eighteen months since Jacob's collapse, and I have booked a restaurant for family, good friends and godparents.

Jacob is suspicious.

'Can't we just get takeaway?'

I laugh.

Jacob has started to enjoy it when he amuses me, his eyes twinkling, tickled that he can still provoke me.

'You'll enjoy it.'

'I don't think I will.'

He sighs like Eeyore as I pull on a clean shirt and cardigan.

There is an art to dressing Jacob if we are going out. I need to do it minutes before we leave otherwise there will be a trail of biscuit crumbs or spilt tea down his shirt, which I will pick and rub at all night. But still, he doesn't make it easy.

It's raining outside and I fear he might have a point.

Who wants to go out on a wet January evening?

Why do I do this?

Why must I drag everyone into this organised 'fun'?

Note to self, talk to therapist.

Anger has to be quashed with fun.

I have chosen a restaurant I think I haven't eaten in before. It is only as I enter that I realise we were here a few years ago. A power cut in a different restaurant meant the dinner we'd been invited to by an art dealer, for a mutual friend, had to be relocated mid-starter. This was the restaurant we went to instead. I have hired the upstairs private room, all 1930s art deco, plush red leather seats and a huge oval table that seats forty. I immediately regret it. It looks like the cabinet office in No. 10. I ask them to bring down the lights, suddenly nervous.

My nod to the occasion is ridiculously big green earrings, which I hope will detract from my still bloated face, and the furry grey tufts now sprouting in faint swirls on my white scalp. I am grey. My hair older than I am. But I am alive. Two more weeks of radiotherapy to go. And more than that, the night is Jesse's and Mabel's.

'We shall have fun,' I scream through gritted teeth in my head.

In the end, it is fun. A beautiful reminder of the life we once led. They have always got on, Jesse and Mabel, and as I watch them laughing and joking with their friends, I am so proud of them, so shaken that we have survived, that we are here, they are here, upright, smiling, nearly cooked.

Bernard, Jacob's dad, says a few words which are infinitely moving – he's a natural orator. He is recovering from the heart attack he had a few months ago, no doubt brought on in part by the months of stress. Mattie, Jesse's godfather and Jacob's best friend, stands up next, addressing the room, delivering words of such love and humour. A perfect assessment of Jesse, our son. Thoughtful, sensitive, old beyond his years, he is, in Mattie's words, quite simply

'. . . a mensch'.

Now Jacqui, honorary godmother to Mabel, is extolling her many beautiful qualities. Eve, Jacqui's daughter, Mabel's best friend, is seated by her side.

'For your tenth birthday you were told you could have your ears pierced. Everyone was getting it done. It was almost a rite of passage. But you decided it wasn't for you. You have not followed the crowd. You've known what's right for you, and you have stood your ground.'
Mabel, absolutely her father's daughter, kind and totally herself, listens, beaming as we cheer and clap, and our irreplaceable friend Eliza, Mattie's wife, plays *Better Together* by Jack Johnson, on the piano, a song special to

us, but which I see few really know. Jacob sings along loudly, oblivious. And as we watch Jesse and Mabel blow their candles out, I feel Jacob's hand in mine, squeezing it tighter. I turn with surprise.

'Well done, babe.'

Babe . . .

And he's awake.

11

It is March. I have *The Caretaker* in my kitchen.

'I told him what to do with his bucket. Didn't I? You heard. Look here I said, I'm an old man . . .'

Jacob is playing the part of the old tramp, Davies, a loud and opinionated racist in Harold Pinter's play. I think 'this is going to be a stretch'. Weekly now, Jacob and his father, sometimes with my mother, sit down and do play readings, either face to face or via Zoom; Jacob giving his all to Algernon or breathing life into *What the Butler Saw*. Like music, Jacob throws himself into these parts with such earnestness it pains me. Today, Bernard is offering direction from an iPad on the kitchen table, a long white table, against a vertical wall of pale white wood, where Jacob is concentrated, barely looking up, on his script. He enjoys these sessions, flicking between accents and character, coming to life in a way he doesn't in normal conversation.

I film him, covertly. Jesse's shoulder just out of frame, absorbed in doing a Sudoku close by, having taken on the strange pastimes of his father in this new life. When I look back over the footage later, I see halfway through I have flicked the camera the wrong way, capturing the glass ceiling and the sky above. A plane etching across the blue is underscored by Jacob's voice, playing Davies:

'I mean we don't have any conversation, you see. You can't live in the same room with someone who . . . who doesn't have any conversation with you?'

A few weeks before this, Jacob is sitting reading the newspaper, again on his iPad, at his usual spot on the orange bench, to the left of the kitchen table. As he slowly and diligently swipes the pages, checking in on football scores and Spurs, I notice a photo of us. An iPhone 'on this day' memory, flashing up in the corner of the screen. A random image of the two of us, on some cold March morning many years ago, his arm around me. We are laughing, trying to out-hug one another. I am curious to know what he thinks of it. Admittedly the woman in the photo is a million miles away from how I look now. But there are days when his silence, beyond the odd platitude that he answers in response to a conversation—

'Thank you . . . Brilliant . . . There's no Crunchy Nut
. . . The box is empty.'

. . . is just too much to take.

Out of desperation, the same desperation that provoked the whole gifting of inanimate vegetables, whilst riding past him in a wheelchair at the hospital, I goof around, disappearing behind the kitchen island, then reappearing as if going up and down an imaginary staircase or elevator. I dive into the fridge then back out again, then back in again as if grappling with a shark in one of the vegetable drawers. Jacob ponders on this, blank faced and nonplussed, a little embarrassed for me, then goes back to his football scores. I crank it up, attempting a kind of exaggerated Marcel Marceau, pointing to the image of me on

243

the iPad screen and then to my face, then the photo again. He doesn't rise to the challenge.

But as I turn away, pick up his breakfast plate, tell myself to let it go, let him go, that it's futile and pathetic, suddenly, through the silence, from deep within, from far away, a signal is sent from the planet Jacob now inhabits. A single line, as the rope is thrown, head down at first, not looking at me, but . . .

Say something. Say something.

'Yes—'

He looks up.

'. . . I'm beginning to think there might be similarities.'

And that's when it happens. I can visibly see it. Jacob is trying, more than trying, accepting that there is no point in fighting it anymore. The 'evidence is overwhelming': something he will say to Dr D when they meet next.

I am she.

She is returned.

All hail, the real Abi Morgan is back.

Funny that?

There's no big hurrah. No grand reunion. No emotional embrace.

'That won't cut it in the movie,' I note to self.

I load the dishwasher. He carries on reading.

Outside it starts to rain.

I should feel happy.

Yet Dr D's words circle in my brain. I have already been told that the Capgras is set to stay, so any change will simply be because it will—

'. . . become less useful to him . . .'

And it has. It does.

Even so—

. . . Jacob wants to play.

In February, Jesse and Mabel surprise us by booking our favourite restaurant for lunch. Valentine's. My heart sinks a little. This could be awkward. I have a feeling we are not one another's ideal date. But I dutifully get him dressed, cancel the carer for the day. We go to Luca, on St John's Street, a discreet Italian, with a back room made of glass that makes it feel you are outside even when you are in. We feast on parmesan fries and steak. Jacob nearly chokes on the steak. At first, I think he's trying to say something, but as his face goes red, then purple, then a strange blue colour, I search for a waiter. It reminds me of the way I call Jacqui first, all those months ago now, not confident I can deal with the emergency myself. But I do.

Everyone carries on eating as I go behind him, smack him hard between the shoulder blades. When this fails, I shove my fingers down his throat, hook my middle digit around a large piece of fatty steak, and pull it out, like a conjurer retrieving silk bunting. It seems to go on forever. He breathes. I sit back down, tears smart. The couple behind look back at us, nervous, offering rictus smiles. I nod back apologetically, already playing out their conversation, as they say goodbye, go back to their other lives.

'Do you think they were on day release?'

Why is disability so humiliating? Why is human fragility something I am so embarrassed about? I hate myself for even feeling this. But mainly, mainly I am glad he is still alive. For a split second, I genuinely thought this was it. It's all I could think, as I was smacking him hard on the back.

'There are worse places to go.'

Dignity restored, Jacob will calmly cut the piece of steak that has nearly killed him and eat it.

'Do you know why we're here today, Jake?'

'Not really,' he replies, demolishing polenta cake.

In the corner, an older suited man I decide is a publisher or something in the city, has moved from his seat and is becoming increasingly amorous with a young woman, a third of his age. He's wearing a wedding ring. She is not. I am surprised at my own prurience. I tap into the notes on my phone and slide it over to Jacob, his eyes tracking along the line I have just written.

Mistress hour. This is when those married meet their other date.

You smile, slide the phone back, eyes twinkling.

'Where is she then?'

Humour is the great weapon in a growing ennui that we fight each day. For the most part, Jacob is still silent, 5 per cent of who he was. This is an improvement on the 3 per cent he seemed set at a few months ago. Sometimes it feels as though I am pedalling a dynamo on a bicycle, trying to keep the lights on.

'Jacob, do you want the bathroom?' I offer, the usual mantra before he goes to bed. He stands, hovering a little at the bottom of the kitchen stairs, trying to work out if he takes a right to the loo. Or risk it and go straight up.

'These are the big decisions.' He ponders.

Then swinging to the right, he says,

'I'll give it a try.'

When the lights switch on, it is like electricity crackling through the water that is the rest. The blank 95 per cent, the great ocean of damage, or dark galaxy, I sometimes imagine him floating in. For a minute it creates the illusion that he is absolutely himself, he is absolutely there.

And then the lights go out again.

And he is gone.

And I have to start pedalling again.

It reminds me of a lot of actors I have met on film sets. Not all, but the greats are often silent, mulling over lines, lost deep within the character that they are inhabiting. I often become lifelong friends with producers and directors, but actors less so. Actors and writers brush through one another's lives, often vividly, but then move on when a show ends or life takes on a new relevance. I don't know why it is. Maybe it's the nature of an actor's brilliance that they come in, burn bright and then leave, always preserving that other part of themselves. The one that builds friendships, seals lifelong relationships. Or it could be just me. Either way, perhaps that's why I love them so much, the nature of the relationship you form, the impermanence. I worked with one actress in her New York apartment for a couple of days, discussing scenes and honing lines with her and the director for a movie. In the evening she cooked us dinner. The only time she ever asked me a question about myself was on set, dressed in full costume and in the voice of the character.

'Abi, how are the children?'

As if being someone else had freed her to be herself.

It often feels as though Jacob is mulling over lines

lost deep within the character, and there are days when he does not recognise us, his fellow cast members. And yet he is getting better at hiding it. Later, much later when I have almost forgotten that he forgot me, it will chill me in a Zoom with Dr D when he reveals, post a conversation with Jacob, that there are still days Jacob 'doesn't know who you are'. In my mind you whisper in my ear,

'Fake it to make it, babe.'

One day I am preparing to go out to work; you come down the stairs with Amina, newly washed and dressed. You are smiling, and you put your arms around me and kiss me on the lips. I pucker my mouth, flat like a muppet, not quite sure how to respond. Not because it is not welcome, or because I don't love you. But the love has changed, is changing, and I don't know exactly into what.

'The problem is there's only one word for love.'

I explain to Steve, my friend, stomping across the heath on one of our early morning weekend walks. It is inadequate to capture the fluctuating state in which our relationship oscillates. The love I have for Jacob is in part like the love I have for a child. I feel the same contentment at the end of the day, when I know he is sleeping and safe, and clean and happy, that I felt with Jesse and Mabel, when they were small and in bed. All is well. And yet all is not well. I can find no one who has lived in this state. Except the elderly, or friends who are witnessing their parent's dementia and deterioration. There are obvious parallels. I mention this to Jacob's neurologist—

'Yes, but dementia is all about degeneration. Brain injury is about repair.'

I meet up with a very nice woman, a hugely talented actress who has had her own heartbreak. Her husband, now her ex-husband, struggled with memories following a sudden illness. She is brilliant, and yet I think I see in her what I see in myself. The constant turning of the box, trying to figure out the shape, see a way in, come to terms with it, I suppose. But I meet no one whose partner has wholly denied their existence.

Before my surgery, way back in November, I go to my local jewellers and asked them to cut off my rings.

'Divorce?' the jeweller asks.

I shake my head.

'No, fat fingers.'

A thin band of diamonds from Tiffany's on my right hand and a cheap piece of platinum with a speck of a diamond that Jacob bought me a couple of months into dating, with the promise of more to follow and which I have never taken off. The Tiffany band came sixteen years later on a random birthday, unexpected. Now I look at them both, held in a china box, the handle of the lid a small goldfinch, which Sophie, my sister-in-law, gave me for Christmas, wondering what to do with them. The bands cut, the gap now wide, interrupted, like our relationship.

Once, a few years ago, I got the scent of an emotional affair. A young actress Jacob had been working with, smart, funny, intense. I met her briefly in a restaurant after some matinee. She came late to the table, but I noted the way she casually ate from his plate. Putting it together with the calls that started punctuating our lives at odd times of the day, my rage was intense, despite his protests.

'I'm not having an affair.'

He'd wearily reply, usually as he was getting out of the shower and I lay in bed.

'You're going to,' I'd reply, nonchalant, whilst internally plotting revenge.

"How can you be so certain?' he offered, pulling on a sweater, his beard still wet.

'Because she's me, was me when we first met, a fuck up. With better hair.'

One day, on the day the country voted for Brexit, he picked me up in Highgate, and drove me to my office. We drank take-out coffee and mourned and worried ourselves that Trump would win next. I complained he was driving too fast and to watch out for speed cameras, our conversation interrupted by her call. Unthinking he answered, her voice ringing out over the speaker. She spoke for several minutes, raging against Cameron, and barely drawing breath.

'Can I call you back, I've just got Abi next to me?'

Instantly, she hung up, murmuring apologies. The terror of discovery in her voice made the hairs on the back of my neck prick up. Later, I found a receipt, lunch for two in a Primrose Hill restaurant – they'd met later that day – dropped out of his pocket.

Calmly, I told Jacob that, whatever it was, it was a deal breaker.

He never saw her again.

I now think they were just friends, something I put to the test when a text from her pops up on his cellphone in the early days in rehab. A few words, simple and straight to the point.

Are you awake?

By awake, she means out of the coma.

Jacob is sitting in bed, dressed, in a food-stained T-shirt, taking his morning medication, which is late. Scrolling back through his phone I see he has inadvertently called her. It reveals a lot, as he rarely picks up his phone, just eyes it occasionally, suspicious more than curious. But somewhere, somehow, sitting, listening to the cries and shouts, amidst the long, lonely hours in rehab, it was her name he scrolled to, dialled. I don't know what he said, or even if they spoke, but his call, I presume missed, is what prompted this text.

'Do you want to speak to her?'
He shrugs, drinking the glass of thick laxative he has to take each day.

'Might be nice.'
'Right,' I reply. 'Because she's your girlfriend?'
'No.' He looks aghast.
'Never?' I push.
'Never,' he replies.
'So you never slept with her?' I ask again.
He grimaces. I'm not sure if it's the question or the last dregs of the laxative.

'Never.'
And finally, I believe him.

I am ashamed of how generous Jacob was, how far he let me roam, as was my right. But there were many late nights with actors poring over scripts, early morning calls and weekends spent working with directors, sometimes with directors with notorious reputations. Never once did he challenge my fidelity. And when he did, it was always with the brilliance and kindness of a friend. Once, post a wrap party on a film, I had flirted – something I am bad at – with an actor, offering to read anything he had written. In response he had sent me something pronto, which I read the next day, with the plan that we'd meet to discuss it. It was a racy short story, well composed, but at the heart of it was a seduction of a short, dark-haired, brown-eyed woman who I took instantly to be myself. Mortified, I went running to Jacob, appalled that I had somehow strayed, somehow encouraged this fantasy.

'And do you like him?' he asks, as we sit having breakfast.
'He's interesting . . . He's attractive,' I reply.
'Then go have a drink with him, look him in the eye and show him you're not afraid of the flirt. If you want to go out with him again, maybe then we have a problem.'
He resumed eating breakfast.

But I didn't, and a week later we laughed, Jacob and I, over an embarrassing detail I had overlooked. The aforementioned story had been written several months ago, way before the actor had even met me, and had already been published in a newspaper.

'Donut.'

He giggled, gripping my hand, I like to think with relief. But in fact, it was me who was relieved. That he was there, that Jacob was in my court. Jacob didn't question for a minute that someone could run home and instantly write a story about me, an arrogance in me that now makes me cringe. He had absolute faith that someone else could fall for me. Even when I often had little belief in myself, he always thought it possible. I have always told myself Jacob's love for me was a one-off, a fluke, miraculous. Even though he would always say,

'Look who's the winner here, honey.'

It took years to realise he was talking about himself, not me. Always by my side, building me up, pushing me forward, proud of me. Ecstatic when I won, indifferent when I lost.

'It's all shits and giggles, Abi.'

My father left my mother when I was thirteen, a few months younger than Mabel is when her dad collapses. It haunts me. What it will mean, their dad's absence? Which is aching and difficult. So difficult for them. For Jesse and Mabes.

On the worst days, I remember when I met Jacob, the first man who I think truly loved me. The first man who truly knew the good and the bad. We could see one another across a room at a party and know when one or the other of us needed to escape. During the small victories, a moment of pride at a parents' evening, the squeeze of a hand, the side look that said, 'You . . . Me . . . Shared DNA . . . Hooray . . .' The losses, when another film has gone belly up after years working on the screenplay—

'Londis?'

'Londis,' I'd reply.

And we'd go and buy the food of our childhoods, Heinz beans and tinned spaghetti rings and fish fingers, to be consumed in front of a film, on the sofa, together.

'Love you, Mr K.'

'Love you, Mrs M.'

Find someone who sees you, I want to say to them. If anything, what I hope for my children is love, friendship, whoever it is with.

Man, woman, fish.

And this is where I see we are inextricably tied, Jacob and me. Our vows woven into each of our children, every memory, every story, our commitment to one another, often questioned, but unwavering. I think of that angst-ridden flight from Toronto, all those years ago, when I found out I was pregnant.

'Isn't it fantastic?'

He was twenty-seven.

He must have been terrified.

He barely knew me.

Once, when he was feeling unwell, months before his collapse, we are lying on the bed in Italy, full from too much pasta and sun, when he turns and says to me,

'You can do this, you know. Even if I'm not here.'

I had sobbed, held him tight, knowing even then, despite the lightness of his delivery, he had meant it. He had always told me he wouldn't live past fifty.

But he did live.

He does live.

I want him to live.

'You're happy you survived, Jacob?' I ask him one day, watching *Friends* on repeat again.

'Yeah.'

His response delivered with a look of such horror I suspect he worries I've doctored his tea.

When I first thought of telling this story it was as a play. And in the play, I consider playing myself. It's brief. But I surprise myself. My desire to be up on stage. A sickening flash of vanity. To tell my . . . our . . . his story. In truth

I struggle with whose story this is. Because when I speak to Dr D about what he thinks about me making a play with Jacob,

For Jacob.

About Jacob.

About what will happen . . . has happened to Jacob . . .

And us. And me.

He says . . .

'Well, I suppose it could be interesting if Jacob could be an agent in it. If the scaffolding wasn't so tight around him that—'

This conversation happens via Zoom. He is sitting in his house and I am sitting in mine. I can hear children far off. Not mine, and today he's not wearing the drainpipe trousers or the boots that make me think of Ray Davies. Today he's in his natural habitat. He doesn't live in London. There are fields or definitely green trees, beyond French windows. He has a grey sofa and distressed walls, which I think is ironic for a man who knows so much about distress. I jump in quick, cutting him off.

'Do you mean as long as Jacob isn't just being moved around a stage?'

I can't remember if he answers. But let's say he says yes and it's in the ballpark, in the region of,

'Yes. That he has some agency, I suppose.'

Agency. It's a word that runs through the spine of our life now.

'To give Jacob agency.'

The goal of the therapists, working with him every day.

'He has no agency.'

When I'm angry, when I need more from him, when I am lamenting over coffee with a friend, I bemoan,

'Just to get a decent argument from him. Just to get some agency.'

Words often spoken by those who love him most, friends who want back the sparring they used to enjoy. All of us are longing for some arousal, some initiation, some drive, some agency.

Ironic, as he had not long signed with a new agent, a good agency.

And I suppose this is why I am doing this. Beyond the fact that it makes a good story. Beyond the anticipation of someone reading this. Beyond the kick I get when at a dinner party the conversation falls silent and someone asks something innocuous, like—

'So what have you been up to?'

And I tell them, I tell them the story and then hear that now familiar hum of genuine, absolute shock and discomfort. Beyond all of this, it was, is, a need to tell this story. But I can pinpoint the moment when I realised that I needed to salvage something from this. A few months earlier, I go to say goodbye to Jacob as I do most mornings, usually in a rush, trying to get kids off to school while downloading to a carer as I go out and they come in. He's sitting at our kitchen table, staring blankly over his cereal, waiting for his day to be laid out for him, to be told what to do.

'I'm going to work now, love,' I say.

And without turning his head he replies,

'I wish I could come with you.'

I wish he could come with me too. I think about it, run it by Jesse and Mabel. They are used to their mother pitching ideas. A story that can be read, might be screened, could be performed. That Jacob could be in, that would give him some agency. Mabel sweetly offers her recordings, and though I have hungered, with the curiosity of every mother who would like a window into the secret world of her daughter, to hear what she said over the 443 days Jacob was in hospital, those conversations to and for her father, they are precious and private and for her to tell one day, if she wishes.

By the end of the week, the fantasy has grown bigger. I have Olivia Colman starring, obviously playing me. Maybe even Meryl Streep playing my mother, if she is free. The entire audience up on their feet, Jacob, ukulele in hand, playing along to the theme tune of *Friends*. By the end of the month, I have spoken to a major London theatre, and we have already won an Olivier. Then it's Broadway, which of course will inevitably mean we are fending off Critics' Circle and Tonys. Eventually I calm down my fame-hungry whore and put her back in her box.

She is despicable, always lurking.

She would sell her own grandmother on a bad day.

I fly to New York for a few days with Mabel. We walk along the Highline, and take photos bleached by a cold sun, retracing this beautiful, once-upon-a-time train track, edged with views of a grey Hudson. One day, we make a pilgrimage to Milk Bar, the mecca of 'Crack Pie' as seen on *Chef's Table*, one of Jacob's favourite shows, a love of which he has bequeathed to Jesse and Mabel. It's a dessert heaven founded by Christina Tosi, surprisingly slim for a chef who has created the Compost Cookie and Cereal Milk soft serve. We eat so much we make ourselves sick, and then realise we are late for the first night of a new revival of *West Side Story*, a breath-taking retelling by avant-garde director Ivo van Hove. We run across town, in boots that hurt Mabel's feet so much I swap shoes with her in Times Square. From the first moment the Jets and the Sharks face off on a wide, brutalist set, we are hooked. My skin prickles with the thrill of it. It's that or the Crack Pie.

This is theatre meets film, huge screens project the interior worlds of a 7-Eleven store and the sweatshop Maria works in. Much of the original choreography has been discarded, but it is thrilling, despite some critics' later disapproval. We love it. Mabel is a street dancer, only sixteen but she's teaching the younger classes at the weekends, and it gives me such a kick to see her beaming, gripping my hand.

We are happy.

I had forgotten we could be happy.

I once got dumped by a man I had hopeful plans for. My revenge was to write his exit speech in a play and invite him to the first night. If I can write this, make something of this, not simply because it happened, but because it might be a story worth telling . . .

For Jacob.

For Jesse and Mabel.

For me.

For someone like me, who Googles at night needing to find

someone who gets the aching terror of the person they love hanging between life and death.

. . . it will be something.

And I just can't carry it around anymore. It weighs too heavy. There are days where I feel it is killing me.

I read up about writing anything personal.

First rule – Don't make it therapy. Nobody wants to hear therapy.

Second rule – Put the reader in your shoes . . . Really? Will they want to be? . . . OK.

Third rule – Employ elements of fiction to bring your story to life.

I fall asleep before I get to the fourth . . .

And then on the last night in New York, Mabel is sick. We are at dinner with friends, flying back the following day. A couple of weeks later, she has a cold, so bad I take her to the doctor. She has lost her sense of taste and smell. There is fluid on her lungs, but the GP, an elderly woman I have not met before, reassures us and sends us away with antibiotics. I speak to my sister-in-law Deb a few days later – Mabel is recovered – and she tells me how worried her sister is.

'About what?' I reply.

'Haven't you heard of this flu thing . . . ?' she offers, surprised.

'Huh,' I offer, only half listening.

'Corona?' she says.

'Oh that . . .' I reply, 'I don't think it's anything to worry about.'

12

Jacob is wearing another ill-fitting T-shirt.

This time with a rainbow, etched with the words 'Thank You NHS'.

I have bought several and forced my kids into wearing them as we bang on saucepans with wooden spoons and clang lids together on our front doorstep, as they do in the rest of the street. All clapping and making a hullabaloo for the overstretched NHS. Later, a neighbour will send me a photo of us. It makes me laugh for days. We look like some mad group of Hare Krishna, making a run for it with the silverware.

It is April and we are in lockdown. The schools are closed. Amina and Daniel, as key workers, dutifully come in each day. We are so glad to see them. They are the only company we keep, bar the bin men, who I have taken to chatting to as they steer the wheelie bins back and forth. We are both meant to be shielding. Jacob is in his element. I less so. He lives his life through Zoom, talking to his mother in Italian, and touring art galleries with her via a virtual world. I have hung a paper rainbow mobile, made by my sister, in our window.

In May, George Floyd is brutally and carelessly murdered. I can't sleep, it depresses me so much. That it can happen. That we do nothing. That we have always done nothing.

I feel shame. Real shame that lingers. We live in a world of haves and have nots. I feel angry that, because of geography or birth, a man can be suffocated in his own street. And then I am reminded that this is London, one of the most diverse cities in the world. It's happening here. Privilege is more than economics. It's being able to walk to work knowing that you do not have a target on your back simply because of the colour of your skin. Life may have changed but the world stays the same. It tips me over the edge.

I oscillate over putting up a Black Lives Matter poster in the window.

Is this too woke?

Condescending?

'No,' I tell myself. 'Wake up . . . wake up.'

I check my privilege daily and I don't like what I see.

I turn over in my head when, or even if, I have ever sent the elevator down. And if I have, was it to help, encourage, nurture men and women who didn't look like me?

In the end the poster won't stay up.

I vow to buy better Blu Tack.

I don't.

I make promises, again, that I don't keep.

I do nothing.

Change nothing.

After I get the all-clear on my cancer, I vow I will be different. Eat less sugar, less red meat. I do none of the former but a little of the latter, trading a burger for Green & Blacks. I will be checked by my oncologist every few months and it will take another five years cancer free before I am, as Dr C would say,

'Out of the woods.'

Ten years before I can breathe and say my odds are as good as the next person. I don't say this lightly, or glibly. I am grateful that I got my treatment over. On the news, I hear cancer services are being cut, beds taken up globally by breathless Covid patients, with ventilators and CPAP machines covering their heads. And those in hospital do not have the luxury of loved ones visiting, as we did Jacob.

The daily death toll is sobering.

I am ready to go back out into the world.

Only the world is in lockdown.

There are other people getting sick.

And all the theatres have closed.

I send an email of support to a morning news presenter I do not know, whose husband is in a coma, battling Covid. I hear her giving an interview, discussing his progress, talking about his comatose state. It is achingly familiar.

I go to the bathroom.

I want to vomit.

'It's trauma,' a friend says.

'I know, it's terrible for her,' I respond.

'I mean yours,' she replies.

Jacob now has his whole choir on Zoom. They are singing something so culturally inappropriate that even Daniel is looking at me with a raised eyebrow. Jacob, blindly banging out the words to some African spiritual with the whitest group of people in North London. Jacob, the youngest in the group by a couple of decades, all boxed into a Zoom call, like some geriatric *Blankety Blank*. I can hear the choirmistress questioning the choice of song.

These are new times.
Changing times.
It is a good thing.
I won't be afraid.
Don't be afraid.
Do something.
Different.

A decade ago, we built a tree house in our garden. 'We built' meaning Jacob oversaw the design and we paid someone to build it. In the end, we spent a small fortune on something that looked a little like a watch tower in *The Shawshank Redemption*, the proportions were so out. It did nothing for our relationship with our very nice neighbours. But over time the mimosa trees we planted grew around it. The twisted pear tree, which supported it, dropped aged fruit each summer, on which the kids would skid. The way back down, a fat, snaking green plastic slide that seemed more appropriate to a sewage works, whizzed children, parents and grandparents down at considerable speed. It grew with Jesse and Mabel. In their teens, they graffitied on it. Jacob and I used to imagine them, when they were older, hidden in its tower, smoking weed. In the end it was only Jacob who smoked, occasionally at the end of the garden, when the pain of his MS was bad. But even then, it was surreptitious, which is ironic given the smell of weed seems to pervade London, certainly pervades our street.

I decide the tree house needs to come down.

The chain on the rope bridge strung between the two

towers is broken. The wood rotten. A piece of the roofing is hanging dangerously. It's a controversial decision when I raise it at the dinner table. I take a last photo of Jesse and Mabel by the flat climbing wall, both of them nearly as tall as it now. Even so, it is surprisingly emotional, watching Jacob staring blankly from his spot in the kitchen, out at the garden, as it is dismantled piece by piece.

'I'm sorry,' I say later.

He just stares at me, teary.

I don't appreciate how profound it's going to be.

But I am brutal.

And determined.

I replace it with raised vegetable beds and a firepit. Neither of which interests the others, but which I convince myself are needed. I am not a gardener, but set to planting, vigorously, Mabel and Jacob helping me. Jacob perched, trowel in hand, on the wooden bench, now fixed under the tree. All part of the day-to-day plan to get Jacob moving, watching the slow back and forth as he painfully scoops up trowels of earth, pressing it around sage and parsley, with great care. But also, I am trying to bring new life into the house.

I threaten to buy another dog.

To add a new heartbeat.

'A new dog . . . ?' Jacob ponders one day, when his silence has been particularly aching. 'You've got enough looking after me.'

Jesse and Mabel should be taking their A-levels and GCSEs, but in the end Covid wins, and after much wrangling we are told they will be awarded the grades that the teachers decree. And again, Jesse and Mabel won't celebrate in the way they would have done, should have done in this life interrupted. Festivals are cancelled, and final proms are postponed. They take it, as ever, squarely on the chin.

The last day of school is around 15 June, two years to the day that Jacob collapsed and Jesse finished his last GCSE. I think we should commemorate it. Everyone else would rather watch TV, aka *Friends*. It's the episode where Joey has found out his father has a mistress and is then berated by his mother for damaging the delicate ecosystem that has kept the marriage in place when he chooses to reveal it. Jacob watches this with familiar intensity, occasionally laughing now. Not the roar of old that I used to be able to hear from the top of the house, but an inward suppressed silent half-chuckle that makes his shoulders lift a little.

I add it to the Firefly list.

That evening, we sit in a circle at the end of the garden, around the new firepit. Jacob, Jesse, Mabel and me, Styler pacing as next door's cat sits on the shed, provoking him. I still think we need to have some sort of ritual to mark this day, and the kids have an idea to write things down on pieces of paper and throw them in the fire. Three things, made up on the spur of the moment – what we want to say goodbye to, things that we wish for, and our favourite herb. I don't know why we do the last. Jacob is perched on a bench that I now realise is too slim to make a comfortable seat, and Mabel, Jesse and I on upturned sawn logs that make me think of fairy circles and Brownies.

My inner monster screams, 'This is twee.'

And yet it is not without meaning. It is rare that we four come together, the very act conflicted, comforting, but always a painful reminder of all we have lost. Despite our attempts to repair, to feel complete, the absence of Jacob, the loss of the man we knew, is ever present. For Jesse and Mabel, on some days, the loss of their father is bleak and terrifying. We sit, almost reluctant to forget him, and let this other Jacob in. But watching this Jacob perched on the edge, trying to scrawl his wants and wishes on the scraps of paper Jesse has cut out, with a blunt pencil pressing softly against his knee, I feel how much we love him, how fragile the little we have of him is. We know how hard he has had to fight just to be here. And how truly frightening it has been, not just for us, least of all for us. Most of all for him.

Every night I put Jacob to bed, and kiss him on the forehead, or occasionally on the lips, flat and platonic. I wish him sweet dreams. He mirrors me, echoes me, repeats the sweet words I pour on him, in a constant loop, a constant repeat, rarely changing from night to night.

'Night, honeybun,'

'Night honeybun,' he replies.

'Love you, Mr K.'

'Love you more.' This is normally spoken through a yawn.

And in the morning, when he wakes, I will ask him,

'What did you dream?'

'Nothing,' he will reply.

And he will mean it.

'You can't dream nothing. No one dreams nothing,' I say.

'I do.' He smiles.

And I see it . . . A flicker of that unbearable lightness of being is back.

When the children were little and I would be racing to

get us out of the door, into the car, he would take his time, quite possibly be just getting into the shower.

'But we'll be late,' I'd scream.

'And?' he'd reply with a smile.

But late at night, as I turn off the hall light, lock the front door bolt downstairs, I hear him talking to himself, as I pass his door on my way to bed. He is back in his dream world, this half place between here, our world, this reality, and the watery, black galaxy I imagine him floating in. And I know that somewhere he is thinking, letting his mind trip. Even if he can't remember in the morning, the cognitive wheels are turning, time travelling, back to the past, the person he was.

'No one dreams of nothing.'

I want to put down what I wrote on those tiny pieces of paper that I scrunched up and put in the fire. I want to say they were wise words, meaningful words, hopeful wishes for an uncertain future, but I remember nothing. Only rosemary. I wrote rosemary. Favourite herb. Later I remind myself this is for remembrance. This firelit gathering is that. An act of remembrance. Of all Jacob was, all we were, we four, this family. But like the tree house, we have to take it down, dismantle what we were, what was so loved, so enjoyed, piling bits at the back of the garden to be burnt. It is preferable to watching it slowly decay.

And the bits we don't need?

Who knows where they go?

But I do learn how easily tomatoes grow.

And radishes.

And beans, too tough to eat.

And sweetcorn that the squirrels climb with acrobatic dexterity, until the stalks bend like willows, and they reach the fat yellow kernels and eat.
And lettuces. And onions.
And rosemary.
All is not lost.
In the worst moments . . .
A.L.L. I.S. N.O.T. L.O.S.T.

In July, the first lockdown is lifted, and we pack up and hurriedly fly to southern Italy, determined to get to our house. Jacob is nervous, seated under his mask, wheeled on and off courtesy of Ryanair. As I queue for a hire car, the kids take their dad for his first crema di caffè, a whip of iced coffee in the arrivals lounge, a family tradition.

Pulling off his mask so he can eat it I smile at him, nose to nose—

'Made it.'

Jacob is shaking, he is so relieved. The mask, I know, triggering memories of the ITU, always pulled off gratefully.

'You OK?' I whisper.

'So proud of my family,' he says absently, licking iced coffee off his spoon.

And when we have decanted Jacob and luggage into the car, and taken our life into our hands, acclimatising to the frantic use of the horn and dodgem-like brutality of over-taking in this country, when we at last swing through the wide rusting gates and up the drive, the lump in my throat prickles. We have got him here. As we promised ourselves all those months ago in MITU. Something I don't think any of us believed.

Jacob moves slowly, brushing his palms lightly across the top of thick rosemary hedges that border the olive groves, walking around the house, gripping chalky walls and touching the pockmarked stone. I realise that we have not discussed where he will sleep. In the end, he opts for the room next door to me, and immediately falls into a deep slumber. I stand outside in the half light of early evening, after we have filled up the trolley with too much cheese and mortadella at Famila, our local supermarket. The fire by the back door is lit for cooking, I can feel my heart pounding in my chest.

I don't know what it is.

I am overwhelmed with gratitude.

I know that none of this is a given.

None of this life is guaranteed.

Now I want every last second of it to mean something.

Even when it doesn't. Even the boring bits.

I don't want to forget that beyond this land, these rolling groves of olives trees, beyond the steep staggered walls of Ostuni, the white city, beyond the flat motorway that takes you from Bari to Gallipoli with terrifying speed, beyond the flat dry grass that catches light and burns daily in the midsummer heat, beyond the flat ragged rocks that edge the craggy Puglia coastline, beyond that is the Adriatic, the sea. The endless grey flat sea.

And we nearly drowned.

We nearly lost everything.

Two heartbeats, faint for a while.

I touch my chest, and then Jacob's, lying in the half light of the bedroom, relieved to feel his and mine both beating.

We have cooked sea bass on the BBQ. The wild cats, mangy and hungry, perched on rocks, eyes glinting in the dark, sniffing the air hopefully.

'You hungry, Jacob?' I say, lying close to him on the bed, putting my arms around him.

He stirs a little, puts his hands on mine.

'Always,' he replies.

Late summer, a few years previously, a good friend, one of my favourite producers, got married in a little village close to our house in Italy. I was invited to the wedding. Jacob and the children stayed in London. A couple of friends, and another woman I didn't know well, came to stay, and it became quite a party. The day after the wedding, when we were all a little hungover, I drove everyone down to Bosco Verde. We parked the car under the shady trees where, after being stuffed with baked fish and lethal iced limoncello at the tree-lined restaurant, we walked a few yards to the thin strip of sea beyond.

The area is notorious for rip tides, and every couple of years someone drowns, sometimes holiday makers. As a family we've swum there often and, on certain days when the tide is frisky, you can feel the pull. Today we eat and talk, and, after, walk to the deserted beach. It is late September and most of the tourists have gone. The young muscular Italians and their older counterparts have left their loungers and umbrellas stacked up, deserting southern Italy for waitering in the North or working the ski season in the Italian Alps. We are the only people. Alison and

Angus, the friends I am with, flop onto plastic sun loungers and sleep.

But the woman I don't know well has already stripped off and is running into the sea. I call out to her – the red flag is up and I have told them how dangerous it can be. But my words are lost on the breeze, and there is a certain defiance, a certain glorious abandon to her, in her halter-neck swimsuit that makes her look as though she has stepped off an Agatha Christie set.

I watch her, dipping in and out of the silvery, churning sea, at one point, her arms raised, back to us, far out, her face pressed into the wind, perhaps catching sun rays. It's cold and yet she is undaunted, fearless. The image is made even more extraordinary because on the way here she told me the story of the day her brother drowned. Profound and deeply moving, I am quietly rocked, not least because there is a wilfulness to the way she now swims.

It is only now I think I understand it.

When the gods look down and fuck up your world, when the map you have laid out for your life has been ripped out of your hands, you are left somehow impotent and abandoned. And with the knowledge that the nature of your mortality is not a given. That life is a process of cause and effect, and however much you might side-step the cracks, stay away from the edge, keep on walking past the open windows, no one can prepare you for the utter shock of the backflip, the left-field pitch, the curveball, that knocks all that you are, all that you have known, for shit. If it's coming for you, it's coming for you. No point trying to hide from it.

They say you should swim across the direction of the current with a rip tide, keep parallel with the shore. If you are able to stand, wade out of the current. Rip tides can flow at four to five miles an hour, faster than any Olympic swimmer. Use any breaking waves to help you back to the beach, let them carry you in. If you need to catch your breath, relax and try and float on your back. Some rip tide currents recirculate rather than flow out to sea and may bring you back to shore.

We got back to shore somehow, we got back to shore.

'What's it like to have everything?'

The last words Jacob asked me, all those months ago, only a few hours before our life changed forever.

'I don't have everything, because you're not well.'

And it is true.

But I nearly had it all.

And that *all* got me . . . us . . . through.

Our children, our family, both mine and Jacob's, our friends, our colleagues, and nurses and consultants, and carers and therapists, my children's teachers, neighbours, strangers, people I didn't know knew us, people I didn't know even cared.

Our dog.

They got us through.

Because you can try and swim against it, you can try and fight it, but for the most part you have to swim across the direction of a current when you are far out of your depth. Let it at times take you, pull you, threaten to drown you. Hope that you get the break of a wave, or the feel of sand under your feet. And then, if you can, on your knees, on all fours if you have to, you do everything in your power, everything with the little breath you have left to claw your way back, pull yourself up, until you are lying gasping for air on your back, with, you hope, the sun on your face.

I have a gang of teenagers arriving. Daniel, the indispensable Daniel, Jacob's carer and man about town, flies over to help me. I don't know what I was thinking, presuming I could do it alone. We pick them up in shifts from Brindisi airport. We hole up in two tiny *trulli*, half a mile from our house, Daniel and Jacob in one; me, Paula, an old girlfriend, and her son Noel in another, leaving Jesse and Mabel and their friends to make whoopee in our place. Early mornings I drop in bread and milk, and check they are still living, have eaten something green. There are beer cans and wine glasses and old bowls of pasta in the kitchen. One day, I see a tangle of sheets moving under a table outside and realise it is one of Jesse's friends, who never made it to bed.

We drop them at the beach, and pick them up, Daniel driving like a madman, music turned up to max, that leaves Jesse's friend Nattie shaking. We buy stuffed focaccia from Villanova, which we eat on the rocks overlooking the miniature harbour as the sun goes down. And drop them at nightclubs on the beach, and pick them up in the early hours, tottering into our cars. When we get them all safely on the plane at the end of the week, I am overwhelmed with relief.

In a few days, Huw and Sophie, and my nephews Fin and Milo, will come and we will cook and eat and swim, and for a while it will almost feel normal. Later, Jacob will come again with his parents, as we all start slowly to heal. Jacob has started to get himself up to the bathroom from the bedroom and I throw away the last of the diapers, something his consultants said I would never be able to do.

Every morning, after breakfast, we help Jacob into the pool. Jesse and Mabel and I, and Daniel when he is here, take it in turns to ease him into the water and then leave him to circle the pool. A slow kind of moonwalking, which becomes a strange doggy-paddle. He won't come out until he's done 100 laps, slowly climbing up to 140; he's in there for hours until his fingers prune, and we have to lure him out with the promise of mortadella and fresh mozzarella for lunch.

He is happy.

The happiest I have seen him.

I ask him how his day scores.

'9 out of 10,' he replies. I'll take that, I think.

In the evening, we watch Netflix, old films that we've loved, terrifying new shows set in dystopian worlds.

Only once can we get Jacob over to the tennis court, hidden behind olive trees. The court that he built, that he played on every summer, with Jesse and Mabel. Now they play alone, the pounding of a tennis ball back and forth, as day rolls into evening.

Jacob watches *Friends*, once more lost in himself, as I cook.

It is heart-breaking.

Always heart-breaking.

But we are lucky.

Can I dare to think we are lucky again?
One house. Four heartbeats.
Netflix.
We are here. We are all still here.

At the end of the summer, we get news from our lawyers that the drugs company who made the MS drug have signed up to a voluntary set of conditions, one of which is compensation in the event of injury or fatality. They are hopeful that Jacob has a good case. It is not a given, but we start the ball slowly rolling. He will need care for life, and, though I have ambitions for him to live as independently as he can, it is a long road ahead. I need to know he is going to be OK if I'm not here. If I can't be here.

Helen, his OT, believes that one day he could manage his way through simple activities by following marked-out migration routes. We have started to explore Apple watches that could talk to him when we are not there and prompt him to get up and move.

Jacob, 10.30 a.m., speech and language.

Jacob, get water.

Jacob, it's 3.30 p.m., it's your ukulele.

Jacob, TV.

I don't think it's an impossible dream. I don't know what remains of us. Of Jacob and me. I don't know what we are anymore. He gave me a bracelet the Christmas before he collapsed. I didn't see at first, but engraved on the inside of the band it reads,

'To my best friend.'

And that's what we are, after we are parents, after we are lovers, after we are family, we are best friends.

Still.

He is still my best friend.

Rewind.

It is the Emmys, Jacob is seated by my side, I am scrabbling to hide my juice box under my chair.

'And the winner for limited series is . . .'

And I'm up. And I'm wearing better shoes. Prada or Gucci. Not Clarks. And Michael Douglas is smiling, and delighted, because the best woman won, screw his writer, screw everyone, he's up on his feet cheering. With Stephen Levitan and Vince Gilligan and Aaron Sorkin. And modestly I gesture for them to sit, gather myself, the audience in my palm, my eyes quietly searching for Jacob, smiling at me.

'Don't fuck this up,' he quietly mouths from his seat.

And I don't.

After I have thanked all the right people, the Television Academy, my agents – who I think I also forgot – Cathy and Maha and Rowena and Kevin, and colleagues, and my mother, my family and my kids, I pause, take a breath, and I say the words I didn't say that day.

> '. . . but finally, I want to thank Jacob, my partner . . . husband . . . partner . . . love . . . who taught me there is no such thing as a pity memoir. There are just words on pages and if they mean something to someone then they are worth saying. Thank you

for always encouraging me to use my words. For taking my hand, for telling me to open my eyes when I jump, because if I don't then I'll miss the view. For not taking that taxi.'

*

On one of the last days, we take you to Guna Beach, Daniel, the kids, Paula and Noel. A strip of sand, edged with rope and faded wooden sun loungers, and beautiful young Italians, their skin the colour of conkers, marked with the elaborate tattoos that they all seem to favour. It has a bar that does good crema di caffè and sushi. And after we have eaten dragon rolls and greasy fritto misto, and drunk iced Coca-Cola, you think you might want to try going into the sea.

'Are you sure?'

Though it is warm, the sea is choppy, with a strong pull. I like Guna Beach for all of the above, but mainly because the water is shallow, and you can walk for some time, with the sea up to your chest, before it drops dramatically into the deep. So we help you up, and take you down the broken wooden steps, bleached in the sun, to the sand below. Help you slip off your sandals and leave them on the beach.

Jesse and Mabel, either side of you, lead you into the water. The waves thrash, but the day is warm, the sky a searing blue. You stumble a little, the waves have a pull, but you want to go on, Mabel and Jesse gripping you tight now, tethering you, keeping you up. I watch you, pushing further out into the sea; you are silent, determined, wanting to go, go a little deeper. For an hour, we take turns holding

277

you, next me and Daniel, then Paula, then Jesse and Mabel again. And we say from time to time,

'Are you OK? . . . Do you want to go back in?'

But you just shake your head. You don't speak, and I realise that what you like is the same thing you like in the pool. The feeling that the water is holding you, the illusion of weightlessness. But it is your look that quietly stuns me, that is deeply and profoundly moving.

You are looking into the distance, a little like a figure-head on the bow of a ship. Like a kite, that wants to lift off, to be caught in the clutch of the wind. You rock back and forth unsteady on your feet, gripping tight onto our hands, and we have to steady ourselves, try to stay upright, against the sea slapping at our chests and arms.

It is potential.

It is hope.

It is the promise of something.

It's not nothing.

It's not nothing.

In a few weeks' time, we will be in lockdown again, and perhaps worse examples of the pain and hardship that have permeated our lives for the last couple of years will be experienced across the world. A sobering, heart-breaking global wake-up call. Our lives to be connected via Zoom, filtered through the eyes of laptops and computers all over the world. Then, more than ever, will I draw on these memories, these days of hope, reminding myself that even in the worst times, there is light somewhere ahead to be found.

I look back at Jacob, face pressed into the salty breeze,

eyes fixed somewhere far off, looking beyond any horizon that I can see.

I don't know what the future holds.

I can't say that there won't be more days to fear.

But I have an image, in this moment, that the Jacob that we knew, we loved, is turning, looking down from his dark galaxy above, trying to reach into this Jacob tugging at our hands. Calling to him, reminding him that he is still out there somewhere, wanting to find his way home. I think back to our conversation, all those years ago in our kitchen, the first time Jacob mooted going into space.

'But there is no promise you will come back?'

'And?' he replies.

'You'd never see us again. You'd never see your family. Or your friends.'

And he looks at me with that smile . . .

. . . that smile.

'Would that really be so bad?'

I take comfort from it.

To know he was never scared of the dark.

He was not scared of the unknown.

Of the uncertain.

And that one day—

. . . one day—

. . . he might come back.

It is March.

In a few months it will be three years since Jacob collapsed.

'So I was speaking to our accountant,' I say.

Jacob looks at me blankly. He is eating a piece of pomelo, newly remembered as his favourite fruit.

'Oh.'

I've got his attention now.

'I think we should get married,' I say.

He pauses, mid-bite.

'Hmm.'

He considers, then goes back to eating his pomelo.

'For tax . . .' I offer.

He pauses, again, mulling on this.

'There'll be cake.' I smile.

And then he looks at me and he smiles.

'I suppose we ought to then.'

So we did.

Acknowledgements

It takes a roll call of talent to bring the greatest stories to light. But to those who lived through this drama, thank you. I would not have survived this story, and the words on these pages would not have been written, without you.

First and foremost, Jacob, without whom there would be no story. No one could have fought harder. Thank you for finding your way back home. To our children, Jesse and Mabel, my constant, loyal running partners, whose teenage life was so punctured. You have shown kindness, laughter and wisdom beyond your years. Now go be kids again. Have fun, smoke weed, say yes to life. And do not worry, Styler will keep me company at night. To my family: Dorcas, the best of sisters, my first reader and constant cheerleader, who picked up the phone and me too many times to count, planted bulbs and kept hope even in the bleakest months, thank you thank you thank you. Huw, my little 'big' brother – the beauty of this book cover envelops this story with the same warmth and brilliance as you did throughout, cooking your way through summers for us, unwavering by our side. I will never forget the strength of your arm around us at the toughest of times. To my sister and brother-in-law, Sophie and Simon, thank you for your love and support throughout. To my nephews, Jack, Harry, Finley and Milo, for your smiling faces around the dinner table, a constant reminder of the legacy that we leave behind. And thanks for the Cards Against Humanity night too. To the best mum, Patricia, who will wonder why she has been left to last, but who I hope will recognise that the strength and tenacity running through the spine of this story was the greatest gift she gave me.

I will forever be indebted to Jacob's family. To my mother- and father-in-law, Judith and Bernard Krichefski, for their patience, kindness and quiet humility when I raged and hated the world, whilst they were dealing with the loss of their son with dignity. Thank you for the play readings and gallery trips and for your constant love in helping bring Jacob back. Sam, thank you for being the constant by Bernard's side. My brother-in-law, Josh Krichefski, for your openness, kindness and unwavering friendship; Debbie, my sister from another mister, who always listened and made me laugh; and her brilliant sister, Jo, thank you for all the kindness and legal expertise. To Ruby and Leo, for fitting into the crook of so much sadness, yet always bringing smiles. To my sister-in-law, Tash, I have known you through the best and worst of times. I love you for your calm and kindness and for bringing the music back into Jacob's life. To my brother-in-law, Luke, for standing steady, yet constantly benign, in the middle of such crisis. And to Eva, whose arrival brings hope and light.

Jacob would not be here without the brilliance of the consultants, doctors and nurses at UCH and the National

Hospital, the very best of the NHS, who were heroes to us long before COVID and who continue to defy the odds. Thank you for never giving up on Jacob and for saving his life. To our astounding GP, Dr Carmel Sher, who always goes above and beyond. And to Orlando Swayne, Marina Basarab and our good friend Baz, thank you for being the calmest voices in the darkest of nights. Eternal gratitude to all the rehab therapists whose magic hands and minds got Jacob talking and walking back into life. To Collette and Diane, who continue to nurse back their loved ones, thank you for your friendship on those tense nights. To Gavin and Emma, for their gentle topiary of Jacob's hair and nails as he slept on oblivious. And to the lady who read to Jacob, thank you for *The Princess Bride*. Daniel, brilliant Daniel, thank you for coming into our lives and to Amina, for the early months. Dr Bonnie Kate Dewer, Helen Harrison, Liz Williamson, Susan Wogan, Jayne Wedge, Tim Smith, thank you for navigating Jacob's body and mind back home. Dr Deeley, thank you for your perceptive understanding of Jacob and for opening a window into his condition and helping me understand. To beloved Rhia, for teaching Jacob how to play the ukulele with his other hand, filling the house with music and bringing his mojo back.

To the friends, of which there are many, who sat at bedsides, both Jacob's and mine. Who cooked, and drove, and sent flowers and never let me down. To Mattie and Eliza, who were always there, through good times and bad. Nick and Ali, thank you for your friendship and commitment to bringing Jacob's waistline down. To Ghiv and Kate, best of friends in the worst of times. Baz,

Damian, Anthony, Jamie, Stephan, Dimi, Nicola, Ali, Daisy, Annabelle, Mervyn, Holly, Nick Sidi, Bill and Sian, Rich, Robin, Meera. Sue, Paula, Lisa, Jane, my walking buddies and confidents. Gaby, Helen and Boo. Ginny, thank you for that dinner party, best invite I ever had. To all my wonderful neighbours, Nicky, Nick, Jasmine, Alice, Anita, Helen, Janet in particular, the honey and eggs on the doorstep will never be forgotten. Lisa, Philippa, Maria, Denise, Jen, Michelle, Sarah, Jacob's coffee buddies and mine, thank you for your friendship when I was most down. To Steve for the walks across the Heath and your beautiful mind whose enquiry inspired mine. To my dear friend and cancer buddy, Jacqui Christian and her family, who truly accepts my addiction to Gail's, and held my hand, despite her own cancer fight. And for giving us the gift of Eve, my goddaughter and Mabel's best friend for life.

Thank you to Vicky Featherstone, mentor and pivotal friend throughout life, who encouraged the play before I had thought of the book. To my Sister sisters and colleagues, Jane Featherstone, finest producer and friend a gal could ever find, and Dan Isaacs, who generously made the maths and money work to ease my life. Lucy Dyke, Claire Batty, Emma Genders for editorial love and Haribos as my world came crashing down. To Lucy Richer at the BBC and Kristin Jones at AMC and my *Split* family, who motivated and inspired me to write. To Ruth Kenley Letts, Faye Ward, Tessa Ross, Juliette Howell, Deborah Hayward, more than colleagues, friends for life. And to Sarah Gavron who, when she advised I 'pop to the doctor', didn't know she saved my life. To Cathy King, thank you for being the best agent, champion and friend who never doubts, and for introducing Eugenie Furniss at 42. Eugenie, thank you for being one of my first readers, for the title – you were right – and for bringing Jamie Carr of The Book Group into my life. David Nicholls, brilliant writer and the first to generously endorse the book, thank you, my friend. Maha Dakhil, Rowena Arguelles, Rob Kenneally at CAA for the flowers and emails and smiles. Jocasta Hamilton and all at John Murray, Millicent Bennett from Mariner Books Harper Collins and Sugar 43, cheerleaders on both sides of the pond, thank you for guiding me so beautifully through the world of publishing.

An eternal debt of gratitude to Dr Sheri and Dr Tan, and all the nurses and doctors at the London Oncology Clinic, St John and Elizabeth, the Royal Free Hospital and Healthcare at Home. When I thought all was lost, you didn't waver in your belief that all would come right. Deep gratitude to Dr Tara Calin, who was there when I most needed her and taught me the value of a good mind. To all the teachers at Highgate School, in particular Karen Norris, who supported both parent and child through the most difficult of times.

Anthony Minghella, thank you for your brilliant gift, and thanks to the Minghella estate for letting me draw on his genius in this book. To the god, Tim Minchin, whose songs lit up the most miserable hospital nights. To all those whose words, be it in poem, play or song, inspired and informed my writing, thank you for generously allowing me to include these extracts. It's an honour to share the same page. To Jan Ravens, for your kindness and insight. To Jill McCullough, for your generosity and friendship.

Finally, to Justine Picardie and the late Ruth Picardie, whose fearless writing and beautiful honesty showed me that there are no such things as pity memoirs, only words on pages and if they mean something to someone, they are worth being said.